Flamin'
Hot

Flamin' H🔥t

The Incredible True Story
of One Man's Rise
from Janitor to
Top Executive

Richard P. Montañez

with Mim Eichler Rivas

PORTFOLIO / PENGUIN

Portfolio / Penguin
An imprint of Penguin Random House LLC
penguinrandomhouse.com

Most Portfolio books are available at a discount when purchased in quantity for
sales promotions or corporate use. Special editions, which include personalized
covers, excerpts, and corporate imprints, can be created when purchased in
large quantities. For more information, please call (212) 572-2232 or email
specialmarkets@penguinrandomhouse.com. Your local bookstore can also assist
with discounted bulk purchases using the Penguin Random House corporate
Business-to-Business program. For assistance in locating a participating retailer,
email B2B@penguinrandomhouse.com.

ISBN 9780593087466 (hardcover)
ISBN 9780593087473 (ebook)

Printed in the United States of America
1st Printing

Book design by Chris Welch

While the author has made every effort to provide accurate internet addresses and other
contact information at the time of publication, neither the publisher nor the author
assumes any responsibility for errors or for changes that occur after publication. Further,
the publisher does not have any control over and does not assume any responsibility for
author or third-party websites or their content.

THIS BOOK IS LOVINGLY DEDICATED TO:

My wife, my mom, and my grandmother, who first proved to me that when God created woman, He was showing off.

My father and grandfather, who let me know from the start that there is no such thing as "just a janitor."

Pastor Ernie Hernandez and the many unsung heroes in my life.

My team at Rancho Cucamonga Research and Development—Judy, Lucky, Steven, Mike. This is your story too.

Contents

Let Your Hunger Be Your Guide

Which university did you graduate from?" someone asked me years ago during the Q and A period after a talk I'd given about entrepreneurship.

I froze. In those days, I rarely spoke about my humble beginnings. Nor had I planned to do so after being invited to speak at a prestigious program connected to a top Ivy League university. Almost all the previous guest lecturers at this business school had been Fortune 500 CEOs or famous professors with impressive pedigrees. Sure, I'd risen up through the ranks of Frito-Lay to become a vice president in charge of my own division at PepsiCo, our parent company, but the reality was that I hadn't made it to high school, let alone to college. Even though I was already known by then as the "Godfather of Hispanic Marketing," very few people knew of my start as a janitor or much about the real story of how I had invented *Flamin' Hot Cheetos*—the multibillion-dollar brand that went on to become the most beloved, top-selling snack on the planet. How was I supposed to answer? Thinking fast, I decided to use the name of the township where I was born and raised in Southern California.

With a grin, I replied, "The University of Guasti."

The grad student looked skeptical and pressed the point, asking if that was where I'd also received my PhD.

"Not exactly," I answered and went on to explain that life had awarded me my PhD for being Poor, Hungry, and Determined!

Everyone laughed, including the student who had questioned my credentials. It wasn't a new line for me and usually got a laugh. But that's because it's true!

With that encouragement, I decided, *Why not?* and began to tell my story, highlighting the lessons, secrets, and practical advice that had revolutionized my career and transformed the fortunes of my family and the corporation that had employed me. More than anything, I emphasized, when you choose to think like an executive and act like an owner, you'll fire up your imagination with flamin' hot ideas that can turn poverty into prosperity overnight.

Now I had their attention. More questions followed, especially, "How do you do that?"

"You learn to turn up the heat on your own powers of observation, and hidden opportunities will reveal themselves. And you know what? It only takes one great revelation to become a revolution."

The MBA students were initially incredulous. These principles of success that had taken me from the poorest part of the Spanish-speaking ghetto, the barrio, all the way to the boardroom were apparently not the standard business grad school fare.

Some of their remarks reminded me of the "Who do you think you are?" reactions I'd received from coworkers, managers, and higher-ups at Frito-Lay whenever I'd dared to break ranks and attempt to present my latest idea to top executives and decision makers.

"How did you overcome the obstacles?" asked one of the students who sat way in the back. "Weren't you intimidated?"

She'd raised the excellent question that I hear all the time, in one form or another, from a range of people who face real obstacles and fears about how to take charge of their own destinies. It's easy to be intimidated. You might be just trying to do well in your first full-time job, but you have a cranky manager who has no intention of mentoring you. Where do you go? What do you do? Or maybe you're hoping to break into your dream industry, but you don't know anyone who knows anyone who can open a door for you—so how do you barge in? Or what if you've been in the same spot for a long time and are considering a career reinvention but are afraid of the competition you'll face? And what about that fear that coworkers, bosses, or customers might perceive you as lacking legitimacy because of your background or because you don't have a fancy pedigree?

The first step to overcoming those obstacles is finding the courage to get past your fears.

"Intimidated? Are you kidding?" I admitted to the student who had asked if I was scared. "One hundred percent."

Luckily, however, I knew of an antidote to fear that I'd found when I was eight years old and growing up on the wrong side of the tracks. *Literally.* There were actual train tracks that ran through the barrio of Rancho Cucamonga, California, which is adjacent to Guasti—a township that had been built in the middle of a sprawling vineyard. People who lived *south* of the tracks, including in the labor camp where my parents worked the fields (and where my nine siblings and I grew up, all of us crammed into one room of the dormitory-style housing), were classified as *really* poor. If you grew up north of the tracks, you were still in the hood, but people there seemed to do slightly better at keeping a roof over their heads and their families fed.

By the age of eight, I was old enough to feel the prejudice that came along with being brown skinned and at the lowest economic level. One of the great injustices to me at the time was that the teachers had two separate after-school reading programs—one for the white students and one for the brown students. Apparently, some of the teachers offered a reward to students who showed up on Tuesdays and got in line to come in for extra reading enrichment: cookies.

What eight-year-old doesn't love cookies? But not all of us got to have them. Why? Because when the education authorities created the program, they set up two different lines and two different trailers—one for the Latino kids and one for the non-Latino kids. Nobody got cookies in the Latino line. No explanations. It was so hush-hush, I only heard a rumor that there were cookies in the other trailer. Every Tuesday when we lined up for reading, I felt a pain in the pit of my stomach. Besides the familiar pang of hunger, I hurt from the injustice of being told: *This is your line; get in it.*

One Tuesday, I couldn't take it anymore. Forgetting my fear momentarily, I left my line and crossed over to the line for white kids. The minute I moved over, my friends looked at me like I was out of my mind.

"Richard, you're in the wrong line!" "What's wrong with you?" "Are you crazy?"

To them, this was a suicide mission. Obviously, I'd be given a serious beating from someone for stepping out of my line. But it didn't matter. I had to know if the rumors were true. Somehow, the thought of a delicious cookie made me forget my fear of being punished. Before long, I looked into the trailer and caught a glimpse of the most beautiful sight. There weren't just a few cookies, there were plates of them!

My friends watched with dread as I neared the point of no return. Determined to convince the nice white ladies of how eager I was to learn to read, I took a step inside and vanished from my friends' sight.

A half hour later, I emerged from the trailer, a paperback reader under my arm. When my friends finished their lesson after waiting in the line chosen for them, they ran over, anxious to hear how bad the beating was. I shrugged and told them there was no punishment. In fact, I said, "Look!" and revealed the contents of my pockets, which the teachers had filled with cookies for all of us!

That day I became a hero in my friends' eyes. More important, I learned a lasting lesson about how to avoid getting stuck in the line of someone else's choosing. As I shared with those MBA students and as I continue to share with audiences from all walks of life, there is already a plate of cookies somewhere that has been baked especially for you. Your job is to get out of the line that isn't getting you anywhere and get into *your* cookie line.

Your hunger is more than an antidote to fear. It can also give you the mojo to get out of the poverty line and into the prosperity line. You can get out of the dead-end-job line and into the line of executive leadership. You can get out of the uneducated line and into the educated line. You can get out of that line where you are not recognized for your potential and into the line of opportunities for advancement. If you don't have the skills or the experience to be in the line you want to be in, if you lack connections, money, or opportunity to open the right doors, this book has been written to provide you with the strategies and mind-set shifts that can help. Even if you do have expertise and resources but have found yourself in a line that's not moving you forward or if you're looking for a new line that inspires you to achieve the greatness that's in you, I've included pointers meant to inspire, encourage, and remind you of your true destiny.

There's nothing wrong with admitting you're not where you want to be or that you are hungry—even if it's just for needed guidance from someone who's made it that you can apply to your own life. There is actually a craving for credible advice that I hear from people everywhere and at every step along their climb. Questions I hear run the gamut from "How can I even get a job in this economy?" and "At my company, you get hired for a job and you're expected to stay in that position, nobody gets promoted—should I quit?" to "What's the best way to find a mentor at work?" and "How can I come up with a billion-dollar breakthrough idea and persuade my bosses to hear me out?" or even "What does it take to become an entrepreneur and set your own terms for advancement?" and "What specific policies help corporate executives empower frontline employees and managers to do more than punch the clock?"

The answers to those questions and more are covered in the chapters ahead. My story of making it all the way from a janitor's broom closet on the ground floor to a top-level executive suite can be your story too, and this book will show you how.

You can start your journey by putting your hunger to work for you so you can move past your fears. There's something better waiting for you on the other side of those walls— solutions to everyday problems that you can offer, ideas and opportunities you have the ability to create. Once I accepted the premise that my destiny was in my hands, the wheels began to turn, first in my mind and then in reality.

My heartfelt belief is that even though we're not all born successful, each one of us is born to succeed. My proof is in the time- and hustle-tested approach that I'm proud to share in my voice and with my flavor, and that I hope may turn some conventional wisdom on its head. I mean, why go along with the crowd when you can throw your own party? My invitation goes out to everyone—from janitors to CEOs. In my hood, all are welcome. These lessons are for you if you're ready for a revolution in your life, or if you're fascinated by rags-to-riches stories or by business in general, or you want to better understand branding, diversity, marketing, and the new paradigm of the empowered worker. The lessons of leadership and entrepreneurship apply universally, whether you are a frontline worker or a top executive, or anywhere in between.

Let your hunger be your guide and see just how far you can go. Your very own flamin' hot revelations await.

Flamin'
Hot

1

You Are Flamin' Hot

Revelations can begin in the most unlikely places. For instance, they might occur in the shopping aisles of a supermarket in the mostly Hispanic neighborhood of South Ontario, California—located just off the I-10 corridor in an agricultural/industrial stretch known as the Inland Empire. A revelation can even take place in the imagination of a janitor, somebody others might consider the least likely candidate to have a major flash of inspiration.

At the age of twenty-eight, I had been part of the janitorial team at Frito-Lay for more than nine years and had already been toying with ideas and side hustles that I hoped would add to my family's much-needed income. The garage was packed with my efforts to develop a signature product. We'd even made a little profit from door-to-door selling of my wife Judy's homemade tortillas and salsa.

Snacks, in my opinion, have always been essential to the good life. Let me tell you, there's nothing like eating Cheetos, Fritos, or Doritos right off the line. It's like getting bread fresh from the bakery. The chips are still warm, and the crispness, done right, can be close to perfection. The famous line in the much-quoted ad from back in the day—"Betcha can't eat just one!"—was no hype.

The whole chip/food production process was basically in my DNA. Growing up in Guasti with a vineyard in my backyard—coincidentally within walking distance to Frito-Lay—I was able to observe the planting, growing, and harvesting seasons. I'd also learned the entrepreneurial story of the township's Italian immigrant founder, Secondo Guasti, who had come to America in the 1800s with nothing but some grapevine cuttings. When he heard about a plot of land being sold dirt cheap, he looked at it and did what visionaries do— *he saw the unseen.* Not the same dry sandy soil awful for crops that others saw. The earth he saw reminded him of home— perfect for a vineyard. He imagined everything he could create from almost nothing. That's a revelation. Guasti and his wife not only planted grapes and began their winery, but they also built housing, a store, a post office, and a church for their workers. That's a revolution.

My parents, grandparents, and other relatives had come to Guasti in the 1950s as migrant farmworkers at a time when the demand for unskilled cheap labor had skyrocketed. They, too, imagined better lives, if not for themselves then for their children and grandchildren. As a first generation American, I never lost my sense of pride that my family's hard work had helped put food and wine on the table for others. Despite our close quarters, we made the most of it—especially at dinner when our family gathered with other farmworkers and their children in a central dining room. The food was basic but hearty and flavorful. We may have been among the poorest families in the area, but as a young child I thought of us as "fun poor."

Once I'd grown up, married, and had a family of my own to feed and clothe, money woes were no longer fun. At all. Fortunately, at the age of twenty-eight, I had a steady job as a janitor and had learned enough to help out on the production line when extra shifts were available. Unfortunately, by mid-1986, it had become apparent to most of the plant managers and frontline workers at the Frito-Lay facility in Rancho Cucamonga that the salty snack business was in trouble.

Sales for even our top brands were down. Rank-and-file workers like me usually didn't get the sales reports, but we could feel their effect. Hours were being cut. Maybe you know how scary that can be, as it is for anyone who has gone through a downturn in the economy—including past recessions and especially the disastrous toll from the recent global health pandemic. An atmosphere of fear spread through the ranks. Workers who usually clocked in for forty-hour shifts saw their time go down to thirty hours a week, then to twenty-eight and still falling. All I could think about was how to create more hours for myself and for fellow employees too.

Then I watched a memorable video sent from HQ in Dallas, Texas, created by Roger Enrico, on his way at that time to being made CEO of PepsiCo. To solve the problem of sagging sales, rather than go to outside experts or only to his food scientists, the charismatic and down-to-earth Enrico decided to empower every one of the employees at Frito-Lay. On the video he explained that he wanted everyone who worked for the company to act like an owner.

He seemed to be speaking directly to me, or so I thought. With production down and all of us in need of more work, it made sense that we could use a new product or promotion to change the status quo—and the sooner, the better. My coworkers and I were hungry. Our families were too. As hourly employees, none of us were on salaries, so any drop in income created hardships like not being able to pay rent, utilities, the phone bill, the car payment, or worse. It's one thing when you have to tighten your own belt, but it's brutal when you have to watch your growing children go without basic needs.

The breaking point came when my shifts took yet another hit and I saw work sink to twenty-four hours a week. There was a feeling of doom and gloom at the plant, a sense of powerlessness. For the first time since I'd been a parent and an employee of the corporation, I had to do the one thing I'd dreaded all these years: apply for food stamps. That went against the resolution I'd made to never return to my childhood of being dependent on government assistance. When I became a parent, I had made a promise to never again live that way or have my children grow up as I had. The generational cycle of poverty that I was determined to escape suddenly seemed to have dragged us back into survival mode.

Often when economic disaster strikes, our first instinct is just to survive it. Instead, as I was going to learn, we do have the choice to escape it and not only survive but even go on to thrive. The lesson up ahead was that prosperity is always on the other side of poverty.

Maybe that's why Roger Enrico's video message lit up my imagination the way it did. He was looking for solutions and so was I. If I could offer an idea worth investing in, that would lead to more hours. The problem, though, was that my knowledge of our business was limited to the production side of things. Once the product left our plant, I had no clue what happened next.

For answers, I decided to tag along on my day off with one of the route drivers. At each of the stops, our job was to unpack the boxes and arrange the various bags of chips on the different sales racks—not rocket science, but it gave me a whole new appreciation for the importance of packaging and presentation.

Our last stop was Ontario Ranch—a big grocery store or *supermercado*, as it's known in the Latino community— and, ironically, the same store where my wife and I did our regular shopping. We were about to leave when I found myself staring at the section right next to snacks, featuring all the spices popular with Hispanic consumers—crushed chili powder, ground cumin, large bags of dried oregano, dried chili peppers of different grades and varieties (from mild to burning hot off the charts), paprika, cayenne, onion and garlic powder, and spice mixes straight from Mexico.

The spice rack had been there all this time, and I'd gone by it or had even picked up items from it many times before. Something different caught my attention this time as I surveyed all the spices and flavors, reminders of the richness of my culture and our cuisine. Down the aisle on the other side was the rack with all our brands of Frito-Lay snacks. None of them offered any real spices or flavors that tasted authentic to people here in my community.

My eyes opened wide. The contrast was unavoidable. That's when it hit me: the time had come to do a chip with some heat, some real spice!

One week later, on a hot and dusty Saturday morning, the family and I went back to Ontario Ranch to do our weekly grocery shopping. As usual, Judy and I and the kids—Lucky (Richard junior), age eleven; Steven, age six; and baby Mike, not even a year old—set out to run a list of errands that we tried to approach as a day-long adventure. Even if there was serious work to do, I figured you could turn it into some fun. What else should you do with your day off?

When we exited the store, the dry heat blasted us, but the wind that blew down from the hills into the valley helped to keep us cool. There was an edge in the air—one part excitement, one part stress. Money was getting tighter. With more hours getting cut at the plant, I wondered how much longer we could hold out before I had to try to find a second job. None of the Montañez family side hustles had panned out. That familiar hungry feeling had started to leave a knot in my stomach.

As we stepped outside that morning, we were tantalized by the rich smell of melted butter and roasted corn on the cob. Our favorite vendor was stationed by the door. The *elote* (corn) man José could be found out front on the weekends whether it was blazing hot in the sun, or cloudy on colder days, or when the Santa Anas were blowing, or the rainy season had come.

This was business, his real, legit operation. All his. In the arena of the freshest, most flavorful corn on a stick, he owned 100 percent of the market share (even if I didn't know what that was yet). He only sold corn, and he made an art of it. At your request he'd add more butter, salt and pepper, along with grated white cheese (cotija), chili powder, fresh cilantro leaves, lime juice, salsa or hot sauce (the wet chili), or other condiments.

Now, a major plus of the Ontario Ranch market was that the owner knew me and would always cash my paycheck (in those ghetto-poor days, I didn't have a bank account), so I had a couple of extra dollars on me. I held up three fingers to José for our order (one for each of my two older boys and one that Judy and I could share with a couple of bites for the baby). Then IT hit me over the head.

Oh my God . . . I'm looking right at the corn and I think—of course! It looks like a Cheeto. Well, okay, a hot Cheeto. The question in my brain spun immediately into words. "Judy," I began, "what would happen if I put chili on a Cheeto?"

Judy did not laugh. She looked closely at me and said, "Tomorrow, first thing, go to the plant and bring home some Cheetos with no cheese. As many as you can get."

Ironically, the fact that Frito-Lay had recently cut down on so many shifts may have made that errand easier. Whenever there was stoppage with the seasoning process, some naked Cheetos would be left behind that we'd have to throw out. If there was a backup, we'd set them to the side for a couple of hours in white tubs with lids and then put them in the trash. Because of the shift reduction, the set-asides were where I found lots of unused, unseasoned product. So I did as directed by my wife and filled a huge garbage bag full of Cheetos without cheese powder and took it home.

That day and for the week that followed, we went to work as a family, setting up an assembly line in our little rental house that soon resembled, in part, the laboratory of a mad scientist, the kitchen of a top chef, and the packing room of Santa and his elves. Judy and I experimented with several versions of her chili—a sauce that uses hot peppers with various ingredients like tomatoes, vinegar, and even sugar. Once we felt the amount of heat and spice was correct, and the consistency (different from salsa but nothing like traditional chili, which is a meal itself) was what we wanted, we were ready to test the homemade tumbler I'd developed that looked like a plastic bag for roasting a turkey. We had to do two stages—first, putting on the chili and making sure the exploded/fried cornmeal didn't get too soggy and, second, coating the hot naked Cheetos with cheese powder and making sure it was evenly and completely, 100 percent, distributed.

The boys and Judy and I were better than any food scientists. Our first batches were wimpy and tasted too bland. We upped the amount of chili and they were too wet. The cheese wouldn't stick. We experimented some more. We had a range of reactions from the kids and my wife and me: "Too mushy," "Too hot," "Not terrible, but something's missing."

A light bulb went off. We were missing the magical ingredient: *oil*! To achieve the right absorption, oil, the golden elixir for all chip making, would act as a conductor. So that's when I took a household spray bottle, filled it with oil, and spray-coated the Cheetos, followed by a second spray bottle filled with the chili. Finally, after drying them slightly, we put them into our makeshift tumbler with the cheese powder.

We improved our tumbler method by adjusting the amounts of speed and pressure. If you're too slow, the coating doesn't hold. If you're too hard, the Cheetos break and you get crumbs. At long last, we got the balance just right.

When I removed that first Cheeto from the tumbler, we all could see that we'd hit the jackpot. "This is it," I proclaimed. We did not eat it. The color—fire engine red—wasn't exactly what I'd envisioned, but it started to grow on me the more we refined and repeated our steps and then tasted our wares. We were ecstatic. Watching our prototype come to life was almost like witnessing the birth of a member of our family!

Before going to bed that night, we made up several Ziploc bags that we'd decided to carefully share with a few friends and coworkers. The response was over the top. To a person, they were a monumental success, and so addictive that the next question asked by everyone was—*How can I get some more?* Nobody could eat just one. This was no weakling amount of heat, though. One friend commented, "These Cheetos are hot all right, *flamin' hot!*" And that's where I got the name. It stuck: Flamin' Hot Cheetos.

Still clueless about how much pushback and outrage I'd soon face from my immediate and upper-level bosses—*You*

did what? Put chili on a Cheeto? That's a sacrilege!—I figured it was time to get an official greenlight to move forward.

A lot of people who had no idea about corporate protocol
urged me, "You gotta call the CEO."

In the executive hierarchy in those days, only the top
tier executives of Frito-Lay would ever have a reason to call
the CEO of our parent company directly. Otherwise you'd be
breaking ranks. This was how the chain of command worked.
Still, I reasoned, the CEO had made a direct appeal to me—
and other employees—to act like an owner. Wouldn't it be
appropriate to respond directly and tell him my big idea?
Besides, if I didn't take action to let somebody in power know
that this solution could actually make a difference for our division, soon everyone could be out of a job.

With that logic, and with hunger for work as my guide, I
took a chance and nervously, against many odds, broke ranks
to make the call. The ordeal made me feel eight years old
again, refusing to be stuck in the line that others had set up
for me and not giving up until I'd gotten into the line where
there were cookies.

"Roger Enrico's office," said the woman who answered the
phone. A visionary in her own right, as I'd later learn, she
was his indispensable executive assistant. She added, "This
is Patti."

"Patti, I was hoping to speak to the CEO, Mr. Enrico."

"May I ask who's calling?"

"This is Richard Montañez. From Frito-Lay."

"Good afternoon, Richard. I don't think we've spoken before. Are you the vice president?" Again, that was because

the only executives who would call the CEO would be his direct reports. Even a vice president would usually defer to a president of a division to call the head of a large corporation.

"No, I work in Southern California."

"Oh"—she sounded like she was flipping through the directory—"you're the VP out in Southern California?"

"No," I explained, "I work in a plant."

She apologized for making assumptions, then checked to see if that meant I was the vice president of operations.

"No," I said, keeping my tone upbeat, "I work inside."

Patti paused, then asked, "What do you mean?"

"Well, I'm the GU." This was basically the giveaway. GU stands for general utility. She asked me to repeat, so I said, "I'm the GU. I'm the janitor."

There were a few seconds of complete quiet. Dead air. Finally she broke the silence and said, "Oh. I'm going to have to find out where he is at the moment and am not sure he can pick up. Can you tell me what this is regarding?"

What could I say? All that came to mind was the truth—"Sure, Patti, um, I have an idea. A good one. I want to share it with him."

Another several seconds of silence followed. At last, she said, "Hang on, Richard. Let me locate Mr. Enrico. Give me a couple of minutes, just stay there. I'm going to get him on the line."

"No problem," I said. "Thank you."

Two minutes later, Patti came back and said, "Richard, thanks for holding, I have Roger on the line for you."

Not Mr. Enrico, but Roger. Wow.

Roger Enrico's tone put me at ease. "Richard, how are you? I heard you have an idea?"

"I do." I got right to the point, letting him know I had developed a prototype of a snack that was getting a great reaction. Roger sounded impressed.

"Richard," he said, "I'm glad you called. You know what? I'd like to see what you've got. In person. How 'bout I head out to the plant in two weeks? We'll make it a priority."

Roger Enrico, by every account over the course of his legendary career, was a visionary. He was able to see the unseen. He recognized something of value in me. He didn't see someone who only mopped the floors. He saw my potential.

When I hung up, I was dizzy with shock and excitement. My revelation was a priority. The revolution had begun.

DID I KNOW FLAMIN' HOT CHEETOS WOULD BECOME THE NUMBER ONE snack of the entire world, kicking off several other products and generating billions of dollars of revenue a year? No way. Was it an easy road? Absolutely not. But in my heart, I did know that I was doing more than creating a new product. This crazy idea, I knew, would be a means of creating a bridge for people to come over and try something that was different, something they would like.

Could a spicy snack cooked up in the imagination of a janitor actually bring people of different backgrounds together?

Without any proof that could happen, the possibility gave me a sense of pride and purpose that I would need to overcome the challenges, obstacles, and twists and turns that lay ahead. Even though I was fortunate to find a handful of mentors who quietly gave me advice, I would also have to face an onslaught of corporate backstabbing—including the time our top food scientist sent out a memo telling sales and marketing to kill the new product before it made it to the store shelves. At several points, I would encounter rampant racism, both overt and covert, including ill-informed remarks about whether I would need a translator when I first visited our corporate headquarters. Not only would I have to draw on lessons learned earlier in my life, but I'd have to fight tooth and nail to ultimately get Flamin' Hot Cheetos and subsequent brands I invented to the public. The effort would require developing a guerrilla marketing strategy that involved spending my own money and taking my family with me to visit more than a hundred corner shops and mini-marts all around the hood in East Los Angeles, buying out their inventory to trigger bigger reorders.

Before I'd even conceived of Flamin' Hot Cheetos, I had to consciously examine earlier accomplishments and lessons learned—including those from smaller ideas for products, innovations, and improvements that eventually saved the corporation tens of thousands of dollars. During my tenure at the company—which culminated in my becoming the first Mexican American to be promoted to an executive role at PepsiCo—I never stopped relying on the power of great ideas. Even when the system worked hard to keep me down (oh, and it did), I kept my faith in great ideas and plain old practical solutions; that's what helped me find hidden opportunities to get ahead that even my bosses couldn't see—basically making a science out of walking through closed doors.

None of us really "comes up" with our biggest, boldest ideas. Instead, I believe, they arrive into our awareness by means of revelation. That's why, in the moment when the idea pops into your head, like the classic light bulb flipping on, you feel that you're seeing something that has been there all along, *unseen* by you before—or by anyone else. You'll wonder—*How come I never thought of this before? How come I didn't see it before?*

All that is necessary to rock your world is a subtle shift in thinking.

Mind-set shifts can truly be as simple as refreshing your understanding of certain words, say, for example, the words *idea* and *vision*. At many of the stages of my success, I saw over and over how the words I spoke had the ability to change or influence behavior. That got me thinking about the meaning and derivation of words, so much so that I developed a fascination for etymology and made it a habit to meditate every morning on a particular word.

One of my favorite discoveries is the origin of the word *idea*, which comes from the late-fourteenth-century Latin as an "archetype, concept of a thing in the mind of God." Earlier we also get a verb from the Greek word *idein*, meaning "to see." From the 1610s, the word *idea* (from the Greek *ennoia*) was defined as a "mental image or picture" or a concept of something that needs to be done that's different from what is observed.*

This inspires us to consider the possibility that an idea revealed to us by ourselves already exists as a concept in what some would call the mind of God or in what others call the mind of the Universe. All this is telling us is that when we choose to tap the resources of our imagination for ideas of doing things a little differently, the concepts have been waiting for us to find them. An idea that has not come into being yet can still be seen in our inner vision as a mental image or picture.

After I had convinced myself that it was possible for anyone to have a revelation, small or large, my next step was to use the power of *vision* in new or different ways. The thirteenth-century word *vision* has meant "something seen in the imagination or in the supernatural." Other than the act of seeing and the thing that is being seen, by the twentieth century, the word *vision* had begun to describe a quality of leadership that commands "statesman-like foresight" and wisdom.†

When you allow yourself to imagine a better future, your vision will show you the way to that awesome destiny. When you embrace the power of vision, you will see that your future is not ahead of you—*it is in you*.

The real secret to finding traction with the hottest ideas is that it's not the vision that counts the most: it's the visionary.

Online Etymology Dictionary, s.v. "idea (*n.*)," www.etymonline.com /word/idea.
†*Online Etymology Dictionary*, s.v. "vision (*n.*)," www.etymonline.com /word/vision.

When you start to realize that *you* are the hot stuff, magic happens. Others will begin to notice. Some will gravitate toward you and want to bask in your flame. Some will be jealous and resentful. They may want to snag your destiny.

There was a time, some years ago, when I questioned whether it was really possible to overcome the odds and achieve the American dream. Sadly, like a lot of us who grew up in the hood or who face daily struggles, I once believed that only a fortunate few ever get to come up with ideas that gain real traction.

Well, let me assure you, I was wrong. Being from the ghetto, by the way, I don't easily admit to being wrong. Even now, when someone challenges my opinion enough, I've been known to say, *"Hey, let's take this outside!"* Luckily, on those rare occasions, my wife, Judy—who grew up in the same Southern California town that I did—helps me keep my cool.

"Richard," she'll remind me, "don't forget, we've come a long way from the barrio."

Exactly. And as every good husband knows—our wives are always right. Judy and I have come a long way. So, though I may still be ghetto, thanks to the lessons I've been blessed to learn and share with others, I'm *ghetto rich!*

Turns out that good things do indeed come from the hood.

Your riches are waiting for you, as they were for me. I am here to reveal yourself to you, to plug in the voltage that helps you flip on your switch or turn up your heat. No matter where you grew up, no matter your age, your background, or your current position, even during the toughest of times you have the means to achieve *your* American dream.

In this book I've chosen the top ten core lessons for achieving your dreams that I've been blessed to learn over the course of my multifaceted, highly successful career, which, frankly, almost no one ever thought possible.

These lessons are drawn from my story and also from the experiences of mentors who have encouraged me and from the stories of individuals I've helped to mentor. All together they're meant to give you the tools for entrepreneurial thinking and for taking action as the rightful owner of your own destiny. My aim is to empower you with the know-how for creating opportunities to be wildly successful and thrive in your corner of the world. Our discussion will help us examine the following indispensable resources that enable you to develop your individualized action plan for success:

* **Your sizzling gifts of imagination** and how to light the spark of your own breakthrough *ideas* by using your *vision* to see the unseen.
* **Your supercharging capacity for *initiative*** and how you can apply it toward understanding the needs of the business that employs you—even if it's not in your job description—so that you can impress higher-ups, potential employers, and yourself.
* **The art of practicing the future you** by fostering both *competence* and *excellence*—sometimes borrowing strategies that have worked for others whose journeys inspire you.
* **The habit of knowing when to act and when not to act** on a hot *opportunity*—and how to avoid having your destiny stolen from you.

* **The unexpected edge you gain** by studying how the most successful *entrepreneurs* dare to look ridiculous, whether launching a side hustle or start-up, or working their way up the chain of command.

* **The ever useful "What if? What then?"** *empowerment* **method for navigating risk** that sets you apart from the competition.

* **An** *authentic* **storytelling approach you can develop** and use to successfully pitch your idea to a skeptical room of decision makers—and why you don't have to influence everyone, only the right ones.

* **Your underused talents for taking on the competition** by making sure you have a *strategy* to rise above the haters and, if needed, a whole new game plan they'll never see coming.

* **Your own pathway to leadership** and the steps you can take to communicate like a pro and connect to others and *electrify* them as well as the marketplace—whether you're speaking up for yourself, reinventing your career, or heading up a company of your own.

* **The true greatness that is already in you** as you forge ahead, without need of permission, living your life with *confidence*, joy, and purpose—even during times when you have to "faith it till you make it."

Many of the lessons I'll be sharing showed me the way to resources I didn't know were already within me, just as I know they are there for you, for free, waiting to be put to use. You have not only what it takes to be more successful than you realize, but you already have the makings of your own flamin' hot ideas. Your own sources of inspiration are right there for you—within your grasp or slightly past your reach, in your line of vision or just beyond it.

AFTER I CALLED ROGER ENRICO THAT DAY, THE UPROAR FROM MY managers was insane. They were beside themselves—*Who let the janitor call the CEO? We don't pay you to come up with new products!*

Their opinion didn't matter. What mattered was how my sons looked at me with new eyes and bragged, "Oh, my dad is something." Long before promotions or attention or more, they'd tell me, "Dad, you're gonna be somebody big."

To them, I was the real entity who was flamin' hot. Everything that I hadn't been early on was going to help me be everything that I would become.

If you don't know how flamin' hot you are, I'm here to light the fire. And there is no better time to get started than now. For anyone who thinks you have to start at the bottom and claw your way to the top, I say, "I didn't start at the bottom, I started at the beginning."

That's where we're starting—at *the beginning*. So let's begin. *Vámonos.*

2

Act Like an Owner 101

There are all kinds of reasons for feeling that you may have become stuck in a job that's not taking you anywhere or even that the system seems to be stacked against you. Many of those reasons are legitimate. There are times when maybe you did try your best to compete for a promotion, but somehow you were passed over and it went to someone less deserving—maybe someone with better connections. Maybe you tried to develop creative ideas that didn't get the attention or consideration they deserved. Maybe they didn't work and you're hesitant to try again.

If you happen to know anyone who's frustrated and feeling stuck—or if that person is you—don't despair! There's a basic solution that can change your outlook and the outcomes of your efforts practically overnight.

The fact is you have more power to change your situation than you realize. You can readily put that power to use once you begin to take the kinds of actions on the job that owners do. It may take practice, but it's truly never too late to learn the fundamentals of what I call Act Like an Owner 101.

Three key lessons I want to share with you for getting unstuck and acting like an owner are (1) Know that everything you were *not* in the past is helping you become everything you were always meant to be in the future. (2) Take pride in all you do, even in the smallest, most menial tasks and put your name on every single thing you do. (3) Become a rock star of *initiative*.

You might be wondering right now why more people haven't figured out how to apply the secrets of acting like an owner if the fundamentals are so straightforward. The main reason is that we allow others to define our destiny—and I know this from personal experience because I once was a person who complained of not being able to catch a break.

Maybe some of the following experiences will sound familiar to you. My suggestion is to go back to your own past and examine their impact, as we are about to do. You may be surprised, as I was, to find out that in order to move on to your future, you sometimes have to first go back to earlier lessons and relearn what you forgot or what you failed to learn at the time.

JUDGING BY STATISTICS, MY FUTURE AT AGE NINETEEN DIDN'T LOOK TOO promising. I had no formal education past the sixth grade, a history in the juvenile justice system, and a reputation for associating with some less than savory characters. Had anyone bet on the likelihood that someone like me would end up as a corporate executive, entrepreneur, business consultant, philanthropist, author, and worldwide lecturer, it would have only been a person willing to gamble on the longest of longshots.

The world seemed to have defined me by the time I was heading off to grade school. There was nothing about me that felt destined for success. No grand ambitions or talents. No major subject area of interest.

Yes, I did have a passion—baseball. Wherever anyone could play in the hood, there I'd be, and I wasn't bad. But without the right equipment or proper training and encouragement, I was only average—not the player to get picked first for any team. School had never been a place where I could excel either.

Growing up in a time of overt racism, I was sent the message that society didn't value a brown child born to uneducated migrant farmworkers. In reality, my father was hugely talented. He could fix anything—machines, cars, you name it. With encouragement and training, he would have been a successful artist, architect, or contractor. Whatever you described to him, he could draw and then build. At one point, my dad had a booming car repair business, but he didn't manage the money end of things and lost it all. My mother was a fighter, doing whatever was necessary to help feed her family. When I think of her *initiative*—a word I didn't know for a long time—I'm continually thankful for all she did beyond the effort just to cook, clean, manage all of us kids, work the fields, always looking for how to add to our income with extra jobs she juggled on the side.

Still, I was self-conscious about my community and my culture because we were poor, brown skinned, and spoke another language. That translated into anxiety—something too many children have to confront, even now. For instance, I have a vivid memory of crying at age six as my mother proudly got me ready for my first day at school. That week we had been notified that I was one of eight kids from the migrant farmworker community in Guasti chosen to be bused to the school that catered to almost all white families. My mother tried to calm me down. With her no-nonsense approach, she teased me—and I'm translating here—*"Crybaby, why are you crying?"*

Because I didn't want to go to *that* school, I told her. Everyone spoke English there. What I meant was—*How can you send me to a school where everybody speaks a language we don't?* It wasn't right. It wasn't fair.

My mother shrugged. *"It's the law. You have to go to that school."*

My favorite uncle escorted me and the other kids to the bus stop at the corner as I continued to complain loudly. "Stop, you're upsetting the others," he told me. Just then we heard a purring sound, and a shiny new yellow bus came into view. The closer it got to us, the more resigned I was to boarding it.

But wait a minute. Next thing we know—there goes the yellow bus. It didn't stop! It didn't even slow down. You should have seen the eight of us kids, none of us able to hide our smiles!

My uncle looked puzzled. Big mouth that I was, I explained to my uncle, "I know what happened. It's a Mexican holiday, we don't have to go to school today!"

"Very funny," he said, not believing me for a second, even as my friends cheered.

As my uncle stood there trying to get us to stop celebrating, all of a sudden we heard a loud *bang* and a *pop, pop, pop!* It was the sound of a really loud backfire from a coughing engine. We all turned around and saw the ugliest, oldest pea-soup-green bus you could imagine. The minute I saw the bus start to slow down, it hit me that we were supposed to get on it.

That ugly bus! Why did we have to go on that bus? If we had to go to school, why couldn't we ride on the yellow bus like the other kids—the white kids?

I was mad for years that the powers that be—whoever they were—had looked down on me. My big clash with the system happened a short while later when one of our teachers asked us to make a picture using our crayons. Well, the school didn't provide us with our own boxes of crayons, and because of that, I had brought the only crayons to be found for free in our migrant farmworker camp. Many of the colors were missing and they were all broken into small pieces. As the teacher walked around the room admiring the brightly colored pictures done by the other students, she stopped in front of my drawing and shook her head with disapproval.

What was wrong with me? In fact, I wasn't a bad artist,

but my coloring was half-hearted. The problem was the crayons, obviously.

The moment made me feel so stupid. It was unfair!

So what was I to do? At eight years old, I walked to a nearby small supermarket and stole the biggest box of crayons in the aisle. A store clerk caught me in the act and, though I begged for forgiveness, turned me in to the owner—who was white. He could have let me off with a warning, but he was a white owner of a store in the hood that sold to Mexicans, his reasoning, I guess, for making an example of me and calling the cops.

The police showed up within minutes, put handcuffs on me, and threw me in the back of their patrol car. The store owner and its management had no regrets. In fact, I was banned from ever going into that store again. (Ironically, four decades later I went by that store and looked through the window at a full display overflowing with Flamin' Hot Cheetos—one of the store's most popular selling brands that had probably kept customers coming back for years.)

The crayon incident made me feel powerless. When I gave the police my address, I began to pray silently that nobody at our dormitory unit would be outside. But no such luck. It wasn't yet dinnertime, but the sky was beginning to darken. As we approached the dorm, I could see a group of women standing outside chatting before going inside to eat, and there was my mom, in the middle of them. The shocked look on her face when the cops pulled up and hauled me out of the car filled me with so much shame and regret.

My mother apologized in Spanish, promising the police

that it would never happen again. For a while it didn't happen again because I never wanted to see that look in her eyes again. Life improved for my family when we moved to a small eight-hundred-square-foot house that my father built, and we went from dirt poor to just poor. The teachers at my next school on the better side of the tracks were worse! They labeled me with learning disabilities and put me in all the slow classes. Actually, I had a form of dyslexia that no one could identify and teach me how to learn to see the words and letters arranged correctly. As a result, I was bored and resentful.

My rebellious side soon started to seriously kick in, especially after my family's fortunes sank again. Even though we lost the house and had to move back to the wrong side of the tracks, my parents refused to let our setback define us. They went right back to the fields and to whatever else they could manage as their side hustles. At twelve and a half years old, I realized that if I was going to be in charge of my own destiny and not let the world define me, the time had come to drop out of school and go to work full time.

In the mornings on the south side of South Ontario, men of about thirty and forty years old would hang out on certain corners. Local businesses that needed day laborers would come by and whoever could hustle the fastest would jump in their trucks for a day of work. Some days I'd get work out in the fields and other days I'd end up being part of a gardening crew. At $1.60 an hour, I felt ghetto rich!

A couple of times I tried to get back into the swing of school, only to arrive in class that much further behind. My teachers pegged me for skipping school and treated me as a lost cause, no longer bothering to try to engage my interest or help me catch up. What interested me most was something they didn't teach—botany! Working as a gardener, I'd learned from some of the older guys, horticultural geniuses, how to be a plant and tree whisperer. No matter how many questions I asked, they were happy to answer. Little did I know that I was learning a valuable skill that I could take to any job. The only problem was, as it turned out, skipping so much school was not exactly legal.

That's when I got arrested a second time—for truancy. The next three months were cat and mouse for law enforcement and me. Eventually they caught up with me, and I landed in lockup in juvenile hall. Looking back, I'm the first to say that these were bad choices. In the hood, though, there aren't many good choices to make—between staying in school, which was a nonstarter for me, and the main alternative, getting out, which would lead to joining a gang and selling drugs. If those are the only options being presented, you are probably going to go with whatever lets you survive in the short term.

On occasion I hear people saying that if you want to help someone, don't give them a fish, teach them to fish. While I approve of the sentiment, I think you have to feed people first. If you've never had to go hungry, God has blessed you. My attitude was—*I want to eat now.*

Going to juvenile hall did not persuade me to go back to school. It did convince me that I needed to avoid getting picked up for being underage and working full time. The solution was to get a fake birth certificate that said I was eighteen—when I was just shy of fourteen—and head off into the world on my own.

During the next several years of on-the-job training, I held my own in the workplace with men twice my age—as a machinist in a parts factory, as an attendant at a car wash, at a chicken slaughterhouse, and at every other kind of short-term laborer job you can imagine.

All of this was while earning a graduate degree in survival education on the streets, not to mention extra credit for riding the rails, getting into more trouble (mostly for fighting), camping out under the stars all over the Southwest, and having my own Latino version of *The Adventures of Tom Sawyer*.

At nineteen, after Judy and I had met and gotten serious and then found ourselves—still kids—as young parents of a two-year-old, I finally realized that juggling odd jobs wasn't going to cut it. Clearly, I needed something regular, a path that could lead me to some kind of advancement.

Lesson number one—the biggest lesson that all my early education had taught me—was that my future wasn't written in stone. What was to come, in my mind, was up to me to write. In the past I'd been given opportunities and had blown them or had felt that I wasn't smart enough to command a good job. Yet I did start to question the messages I'd been sent from others. This was the beginning of my learning to act like an owner by understanding this first fundamental— how everything that I had *not* been in the past would help me focus on the things I needed to do to improve and eventually to become everything I was always meant to be.

On that hopeful note, within days of starting my job hunt, by kismet, I heard that Frito-Lay might be hiring—and that the starting position of janitor paid $3.10 an hour plus benefits. I'd never wanted anything as much as I wanted to have that job. This was my long-awaited chance to change my legacy.

There was one hitch. Every applicant had to fill out an application. In those days I could barely read or write. Thinking fast, I grabbed the application and promised the human resources manager I'd bring it back as soon as possible. At home Judy sat down with me to help fill it out. We went over every question carefully as she wrote down my thoughtful responses.

The next morning, when I handed the application to the HR manager bright and early, he glanced over it and asked, "Did you fill this out?"

My reaction was to laugh and shrug—which could be interpreted either way.

"Hmm," he said and then added, "You have nice handwriting."

You can bet that I've been singing Judy's praises ever since.

The good news is that I got the job and was approved to start that night on the graveyard shift. Not so good news was my concern that they might do a background check. But in those preinternet days, not much showed up unless it was really bad. And there was nothing super bad in my past even if none of it was very good. In any case, when I was told to come in for my first shift, I was over the moon.

Janitor! My dream job. You could have told me that I had just been accepted by Harvard!

Ironically, years later, when I was invited to sit on a board of industry leaders by then California governor Arnold Schwarzenegger, I was asked whether there was anything in my past or my relatives' past that might embarrass him politically. For a minute I joked, "You know, I'm Mexican, and everyone has that one uncle. . . ." In other words, though I didn't say it, I wasn't sure, once again, that I could clear a background check. After all, it could just be that they don't find anything on your relatives because *you* are that one uncle. To my relief, I got the call that nothing had turned up in my past, and I was able to serve on the board.

As soon as the Frito-Lay HR manager told me to show up that very night at eleven, I ran the quarter mile across the road to the fields to find my dad and his dad laboring under the hot sun and gave them the news.

"Frito-Lay? You got a job at the plant?" Going from the fields to the factory was a big deal for anyone, a breakthrough for the Montañez family.

My grandfather was so happy too. "What's your job?" he asked.

"I'm the janitor."

My father and his father looked at each other without expression, as if to decide who was going to speak first. My father, showing respect, let my grandfather give me some advice—words I have lived by ever since.

He put his hand on my shoulder and said, "Listen to me.

When you mop that floor, you make sure that when people there see it, when anyone sees the floor, all the people will know that a Montañez mopped it." My father nodded.

With those words, they gave me the foundation for lesson number two of acting like an owner. As I was to learn, over time, the more you take pride in all you do, even in the smallest, most menial tasks—always putting your name on every single thing you do—you become a person of value to your company and to yourself.

Owners put their names on their work. They stand behind their product and their services. They preserve their brand. From then on, I did the smallest tasks with pride and in honor of my parents and grandparents, for my sons and my granddaughters and grandsons, for our last name. Your last name is not the company that employs you; your last name is your legacy.

This was a powerful mental shift that changed my entire attitude from then on. The third fundamental of acting like an owner was around the corner, and it, too, would be life changing.

AFTER TWO WEEKS OF TAKING PRIDE IN MY DUTIES—SWEEPING, mopping, and buffing the floors to a high sheen—I confidently walked into the office of my supervisor, Jim, who had summoned me for a review. Jim was a strapping red-haired dude with massive biceps from his long hours in the gym after work. He was the guy who oversaw all the areas of the plant that I was responsible for mopping and cleaning.

"Richard," he said, getting down to business. "I gotta let you go."

Maybe I hadn't heard him right. My shock must have been obvious. This job was my future, a chance to put a roof over my family's head and food on the table. For the last two weeks, I had worked harder than ever, doing all that was asked of me. The whole time I'd reminded myself: *Richard, you've blown everything in your life; don't blow this job!*

Fumbling for words, I finally asked, "Was there something I didn't do right?'

"No," he admitted. "You show no initiative." The word went over my head, but when he explained that I would mop a floor and clean the rooms and still have two hours left, I wouldn't do anything extra—so I'd clean everything again.

Taking the least bit of initiative I knew how, I begged Jim, "Give me a little more time, I'll show you initiative." Jim said he'd give me the two weeks but seemed like he'd already decided to fire me.

At home I fought back tears, telling Judy, "He said I don't have any initiative!" After two weeks, I'd nearly blown the one break I'd ever caught. I felt like a broken individual. "Am I gonna be a dummy my whole life?" I asked her.

We did something that was a first but certainly not the last. Judy and I went to the public library, located a dictionary, and looked up the meaning of taking *the initiative*:

The power or opportunity to do something before
others do

If you want to meet her, you're going to have to *take the
initiative* and introduce yourself.

The company has the opportunity to *seize the initiative* by getting its new products to the market before its
competitors.*

What? I could do that! Almost getting fired was a much-
needed kick in the pants for me to go beyond the bare minimum. Everything changed. The next shift, I did the required
regular duties, but because I had time on the clock, I started
to get to know the whole operation, observing how everything
worked and looking for ways I could clean in parts of the plant
that weren't on my regular list of duties.

My schedule's main weekday janitorial responsibilities
included making sure that the different work areas—lunch
spaces, locker areas, and restrooms—were clean and safe,
with garbage hauled off and clutter removed. During the
graveyard shift on weeknights I'd clean the offices, hallways,
and the cafeteria—the busiest and most trafficked spaces at
the plant. That is, of course, outside of the production areas
that housed the different lines. Those I cleaned on the weekends, when the plant was shut down and I could do a much

Merriam-Webster.com Dictionary, s.v. "the initiative (*n.*)," www.merriam
-webster.com/dictionary/the%20initiative.

more heavy-duty cleaning of food processing machinery and safety equipment. We had pressurized hoses, acid washes, and other means of performing the duties involved in major industrial cleaning.

As I started to use my extra time to scout around for ways I could help out more, I was surprised to learn how each of the five brands that were being produced at our plant was run differently from the others. Every night I'd run home and tell Judy the latest discovery. Such as:

* The Frito-Lay standards for quality control were so high, I would see chip rejects getting thrown out for the smallest defects. "What you throw out," I later said to one of the managers, "I could put in a bag and sell."
* I noticed that when supplies and materials started to run low in the different production areas, workers would replace containers that weren't actually empty. But there was no systematic way to prevent that waste from happening. I started making notes about ways to prevent it. No one told me to do it, but to me that was acting like an owner.
* Even though the five products we made—Fritos, Doritos, Tostitos, Cheetos, and Funyuns—were all made of corn, the process and the equipment for each kind of chip was very different from the others. Certain machinery on certain lines tended to break down more often than on others, but the workers who used the machinery would have to wait for a specialist to come to fix it. The corporation lost money every time that person was less productive.

* The most complicated chip production process is for the Cheeto. The cornmeal goes into a die and then the heat explodes it into a Cheeto form. Of all the chips, the process requires the most attention. Yet scheduling wasn't always on top of that.

* At every shift, every line worker had to work in sync with the others. One would control the preparation of the corn, for example, another would control the seasoning, and others would be responsible for moving the materials along. Running those lines required precision and focus, but it took a gifted operator to run the show. I wondered how those skills and abilities were first identified.

Out of curiosity and initiative, I started asking questions, even at times in a way that annoyed managers and frontline workers. My types of questions ran the gamut:

* *Instructional.* Wanting to learn, I'd be direct and ask, "Can you tell me how you do this job?" Most of the time my fellow employees liked being asked about their expertise and were willing to show me the drill for how different chips were made, in minute detail.

* *Operational.* I'd ask a lot of questions that started out with the word *why.* "Why do some operators set their timing devices at slower settings than others?" (Slowing down productivity but avoiding mishaps.) Little details that went wrong in one area, I learned, could throw off all the other areas. Using too much oil, for instance, wasn't a

problem for flavor or crispness but, in my view, it was an unnecessary extra cost. Then I'd compute how much that was per hour. Before long, I was doing high-level math! Concepts that were once over my head in a school setting now suddenly made sense. I would learn to figure out how many fryers were needed to produce X amount of chips a minute in order for us to operate at full capacity to meet our production needs.

* *Technical.* Whenever I observed anyone who really knew their stuff, I'd latch on to them and ask questions that were highly technical and based on science, such as, "Why is a flat chip not as crunchy as one that's more dimpled?" Then, after follow-up questions, I'd research what caused certain chips to have the right dimpling—or blistering, as we called it—to create the best crunch. From there, I'd ask more questions about how certain processes ran the risk of making the chips too flat and not as satisfying.

Initiative inspired me to keep a pen and small notebook on me at all times. In addition to writing down the questions and answers I'd been getting, I also started doing expense calculations for materials and jotting down various observations about how the lines could be run more efficiently and save money for the company. There may be no tool of the trade more useful for acting like an owner than a pen and a pocket-sized, old-fashioned small notebook you keep with you at all times.

Before long, I started to become fairly proficient at the different production jobs. When someone needed a cigarette or a bathroom break, I'd jump in and run their part of the line, eventually subbing on full shifts. Productivity became an area of fascination.

Early in this process, it occurred to me that acting like an owner by taking initiative doesn't just mean doing the things well that you're told to do. It means:

1. Figuring out how the whole operation works—not just for doing your job, but all the departments that interact with one another and with you.
2. Asking questions without being afraid of sounding stupid.
3. Being willing to hear criticism and then making the appropriate adjustments.
4. Taking it upon yourself to find out what needs to be done, and doing it.
5. Always doing the little things with integrity, even when no one's paying attention.

After my first two weeks of using the power of initiative, Jim from HR was impressed and gave me the go-ahead to stay on as a full-time janitor, praising me in my review. I never forgot that close wake-up call. Later on, as an executive involved with training and leadership development, I'd always encourage managers and HR recruiters to educate new employees on the importance of initiative and not being afraid to ask questions. When you hire someone who only does what you ask, that puts more pressure on you as an owner, boss, or executive to remember everything you need that employee to do for you. But when that employee takes the initiative to think of the goals and needs of the situation and handles them before being asked, that's golden.

From the moment I conquered the fundamentals of acting like an owner, I found the tools that kept me from feeling stuck—even when I wasn't always being given the promotion or compensation I would have liked.

Taking initiative pays off most of the time. Sometimes you step on toes. I remember at one point I felt that my efforts had finally yielded a chip with the perfect crunch. In my spare time on weekends, I'd been playing around with different methods of stone-grinding the corn that had already been soaked in water and lime, run through a hydro-jet cleaning process, and then soaked again into *masa* (a corn mash). Once we shot that through a hose into a vat where it was ground between two massive stones, we could adjust how finely ground the meal was by bringing the stones in closer. In theory, the finer the meal, the more it would blister when the chip hit the fryer. If it was too fine, like sand, the chip would be too flat without the right crunch and would lack the satisfaction from a crunch-blistered chip.

The process I used produced a thinner and lighter yet still crunchier chip, so I sent it off to the R & D team, happy to be of service. They were not happy. Their response was, "You're right, this tastes great, but it doesn't fit our spec." Their reasoning was that it didn't comply with the quality already established. In other words—*If it ain't broke, don't fix it.*

My chips with added crunch were not, in their view, "up to quality."

My response was, "Quality—according to whose tongue?"

Apparently, they didn't love my initiative. It was a lesson learned. Not everyone is going to cheer for your going the extra mile if it's seen as trespassing on their turf.

Much of the time, however, being ready to go above and beyond the call of duty is well worth the effort.

I'll never forget what happened about two years or so after I'd started at Frito-Lay when the time came to test everything I'd learned. One night, just as I arrived at the plant for the graveyard shift and made the rounds, I could hear one of the managers barking because his operator on the Doritos line hadn't shown up for the next eight-hour shift. Now either the Doritos line was going to go down or the operator who ran the last shift would have to work another shift. Calls had gone out for someone to come in on short notice but, apparently, no processing operator showed who could take over and run the entire process.

"Let me do it," I offered the manager, who was unaware that I'd already been covering for some of the operators on their breaks. Being trained as an operator who could actually run an entire line—a processing specialist—took a long time. "You're crazy!" said the manager, waving me off.

My actual entry-level job title was "porter," which in the late 1970s was seen as a fancier name for janitor or even custodian. As that manager knew, my main responsibilities included making sure that the offices, hallways, and the cafeteria, food processing machinery, and safety equipment were clean and safe.

I told the manager that others on the line could vouch for me. "You don't have to worry," I promised.

The manager was in a tough spot. He didn't want to shut the line down, but this was *not* protocol. There were other workers who had been trained and were on a waiting list for the spot. Then again, where were they?

"Fine," he muttered. "If you screw up, you're fired."

For the next eight hours—two four-hour shifts—I ran the line with the precision, attention to detail, hyperfocus, and finesse of a race car driver. The rhythm and pace of the three phases of production—(1) processing of the chips, (2) bagging the chips, (3) boxing the chips and sending them into the warehouse for shipping and delivery to the stores—all flow from the timing and mastery of the processing operator who runs all the different stations of the overall line. All went smoothly.

Productivity, as I had been studying all this time, was measured by how many pounds of product were pushed through in a given eight-hour period. A good eight hours would yield something in the vicinity of eighteen thousand pounds of chips bagged and boxed. Sometimes you'd have a breakdown of a machine, and the timing would have to be slowed way down to the point that you'd get only eight thousand pounds per eight-hour shift. In the calculations in my notebook, I had already figured out how much *masa* would be needed on an hourly basis to be able to reach that eighteen-thousand-pounds-per-eight-hour benchmark. I'd noted previously that by increasing the speeds of the machinery and resetting the timing devices, we could push through that higher amount of product. The risk was that if you tried to do it too fast or if the timing wasn't reset correctly, you could have multiple breakdowns. Or you would sacrifice quality for quantity.

Was I going to play it safe or put my theories to the test? My decision was to act like an owner and go for it. Quickly resetting the timing on all the machinery and letting everyone know what to expect for the next eight hours, I was so determined to keep everyone moving without any delays, especially in the seasoning and bagging stages, that I pushed through a lot of product. In my imagination, this was like the World Series, the stakes were so high, and I was like the coach of a pro baseball team—cheering everybody on, getting them pumped about doing the same tasks they usually did. Nobody said much when the time came to go home, other than that there were no apparent screwups.

Later that week, though, unbeknownst to me, the plant manager read the report and called in the manager who had let me pinch-hit, asking, "Who was the operator on the Doritos line?"

"Oh, you know, that guy, the porter . . . the janitor."

"Do you know how many pounds of product he pushed through?" the plant manager asked. Turned out I had well exceeded eighteen thousand pounds by at least another five thousand pounds. The next time I subbed on a shift as the main operator, I set a company-wide record for the most pounds of product ever bagged and boxed in an eight-hour shift: thirty thousand pounds. The upshot was: "Maybe you should ask him if he wants to run a line on a regular basis." (Decades later I heard that one of the youngest frontline workers I had trained back in my day had finally broken my record.)

The plant manager couldn't hand me a job like that. First, I had to put in a bid for it. And once I was accepted, I still had to prove myself in other ways. Instead of giving up my job as janitor, I kept it and then began working on all the lines in second-shift spots. First I was a fryer operator, then a tortilla chip operator, and, eventually, I ran the different lines— working up to processing specialist.

None of that would have happened if I hadn't learned those three fundamentals of acting like an owner. (1) As an entry-level employee, I had not forgotten the feeling of being stuck or limited in earlier jobs and tried to learn from what hadn't gone well before. (2) Even with the smallest of tasks, I'd taken pride in my efforts and put my name on them. In fact, when I set a record for the most product pushed through on a shift, I could proudly say that a Montañez had done it. (3) I'd learned the hard lesson of taking initiative.

There was one more general rule for thinking like an owner that came to me after overhearing a conversation at the plant about job satisfaction. It seemed that one of my co-workers had been complaining about his job to a midlevel manager. My coworker had been feeling stuck in a rut and was questioning whether he should look elsewhere for work. He said, "I'm just not that happy here."

Our manager looked at him and laughed. He said, "If my job was to make you happy, I'd give you Disneyland tickets."

It sounded harsh, but he had a point. The realization for me was that it really isn't your employer's job to make you happy. That's your job. My family made me happy. Dreaming of being able to afford a classic car or custom motorcycle one day—those thoughts made me happy. And what I really learned from that exchange was that you don't have to love your job to be successful, but you do have to love to work. Whether you stay in your job or go elsewhere for a better fit, the love you have for getting up and at it every day will serve you over the long haul.

As you think about how you might want to put acting like an owner to the task for yourself, here are some questions to ask yourself:

* *Have you embraced the belief that you are in charge of your destiny?* If so, great! You might want to give yourself goals that have nothing to do with someone signing on to your plans. Try writing down your daily goals in the morning and checking off your accomplishments at night.
* *Are you carrying around old messages that you were sent or that you sent yourself about never being able to catch a break?* The funny thing is that a lot of those messages lose their shelf life over time and just are not true. You can replace them with new, more positive messages. How would an owner give you a pep talk about what makes you of value to your employer? How would you give yourself that same pep talk?
* *Are you working for the entity that writes your paycheck or are you working for your last name—your legacy?* If you can come up with an accomplishment made in the past, have you given yourself credit for it and taken pride in it as part of your legacy?

* *If you're feeling a little stuck, can you take the initiative to do one extra thing tomorrow that gets you out of your comfort zone in order to act like an owner?* Every small action taken on a daily basis will add up. You can ask a question, read an article or book, explore a facet of the workplace you may never have seen.

* *Last, if you have that sinking feeling that your job isn't for you, can you spend a week just focusing on the love of hard work?* You may get the answer that it's time to seek another position. Or not. Acting like an owner will help guide you to figuring out what is going to be the best use of you.

When you choose to act like an owner, you are employing a mental shift that lets you be the operations specialist of all the phases of your life.

The near failure that almost got me fired taught me the hard lesson that gave me courage later on. When you take initiative and go beyond the bare minimum, you'll improve the odds for succeeding and outliving your lack of knowledge, even your failures and mistakes.

As you begin to act more and more like an owner, stepping outside of the box of just doing what's expected, your habit of taking initiative will inevitably change your circumstances and you. The next step takes you further not only toward acting like an owner, but also toward thinking in ways you may never have thought before.

3

Learn to Think Like an Executive

One day after I'd been at Frito-Lay for more than three years, I arrived at the plant well before my shift was to begin and happened to pass by the conference room where our head of operations was in the middle of reviewing our most recent production, shipping, and sales numbers. An excellent speaker, he had the attention of everyone in the room—mostly managers, directors, and other executives—as he went through an array of data, pointing out where we'd exceeded our goals and where we had fallen short. Fascinated, I took a seat in the back and began to write down a few of the main points he had been making in my ever-ready notebook.

That day, nobody said anything to me about why I was there, but after I'd started to show up regularly at these meetings, some of the managers started making comments, such as: *You better not be on the clock. We don't pay you to sit in on these talks.* They asked what the heck I was doing with the notebook, basically saying in so many words—*Who do you think you are?*

Rather than tell them who I thought I was, I'd reassure them that I wasn't on the clock and that I just liked the way our head of operations simplified a lot of complicated information.

They would usually just shake their heads and walk off, grumbling about how they weren't paying me to sit in on their meetings. Or they'd say, "Fine, suit yourself."

Then I would have to give myself a pep talk and a reminder that all I was doing was practicing the future me. How? By learning to think like an executive.

In those days, I didn't have much of a clue about how executives actually thought. All I knew was that if I could learn more about what executives really did and how they had ascended to their higher positions of responsibility and decision making, I could then learn to think as they did.

Without a second thought, one day I decided to stop by the office of the head of operations and ask him about his data. When I popped my head in, his secretary looked startled and asked, "Can I help you?"

"Yes, I wanted to make an appointment."

At that moment the executive saw me and asked if he could be of help. When I explained that I wanted to set up an appointment to ask some questions about his presentation because it was information that could help me to be better at my job, he shrugged and invited me into his office. I pulled out my notebook and politely started to ask questions about great points he had made, adding a suggestion here and there about how to help him meet his goals from the perspective of a frontline worker. My main question was whether it would be possible for me to get his reports on a regular basis and share them with my coworkers.

"You know, you're right; everyone should have access to the reports," he agreed, as if he couldn't believe no one had ever thought of that before. From then on, he started distributing his reports to everyone at the plant. He thanked me for the idea and told me his door was open to me anytime. The thing that had made the difference was that I had brought him information and a connection to frontline workers. It was something that many executives lacked. He understood that human resources are a company's most valuable assets and that motivating workers would be good for the corporation overall. From then on, whenever I had any questions about operations and how an executive might be thinking about a certain issue, I knew where to go. It was a start!

If you believe that you have more to offer but have been held back in your current position, or that you don't have anyone helping you to advance, or you just want to know how to get past the gatekeepers and closed doors to get the attention of higher-ups, the first thing I want you to understand is that you don't need anyone's permission to begin practicing the future, more successful you. There's no need to apologize for thinking ahead of yourself as you explore the next steps that begin with something I'd clearly failed to do back in my school days:

1. *Do your history homework.* Almost every company, small or large, has a beloved brand history, plus a history of founders and influential executives. When you get to know that history and the contributions of the people who shaped it, you increase your value to the executive branch—whose members, in classical terms, are the defenders of the realm and protectors of the brand. Then you'll be thinking like an executive.

2. *Learn the difference between excellence and competence and why executives should have both.* When you want to get hired or promoted, ask not what the company can do for you but what you can do for the operation as a whole. Top executives not only demonstrate excellence and competence themselves, but they also understand that they need to identify those traits in others.

3. *Seek out role models and mentors who can teach you without even knowing that they're doing so.* It can be very difficult to find someone, especially a busy executive or upper-level manager, who has the time or interest to meet with you, let alone oversee your advancement. That is, unless they discover that they can learn from you too. The wisest executives, like the best teachers, never stop learning.

In the early 1980s, when I was only beginning to become aware of a big disconnect between frontline workers and the upper levels of management, I knew nothing of these three basic steps toward thinking like an executive. The only thing apparent was that learning brand history—how Frito-Lay and Pepsi had come together to become PepsiCo—was like studying the Bible to many executives. Practicing the future me, that's where I started my homework: learning about the early days of crunchy snacks.

AT ONE TIME, THE MERE THOUGHT THAT I COULD WORK MY WAY UP TO the role of vice president of a corporation would have made even me shake my head. But when I sat down to learn a little more about how the corporation had come to be, I did start to see myself moving up to a position with a bit more responsibility. At a time when there were no Mexican Americans who had been promoted to an executive level at our company, I was happy to learn that before the corn chip and the potato chip became household food staples, the individuals most credited with their invention were not from mainstream America at all. The corn chip originator was a Mexican street merchant, while the man said to have invented the potato chip was a half African American/half Native American chef in a fancy resort restaurant.

That was the backdrop for the story of the entrepreneur and executive who first recognized massive potential for corn chips: Charles Elmer Doolin. He got his start during the Great Depression with a string of businesses, including a confectionary in San Antonio. Doolin was always on the lookout for other people's innovations—in particular some kind of a corn snack he could sell at his shop that would not have to be sugar laden. Tortillas had no shelf life, so he wasn't sure what kind of corn snack would do.

Nothing much turned up until one day when he came across a street vendor from Mexico outside a gas station, where he was selling his wares—corn chip–like fried bits made out of extruded *masa*, plopped in hot oil, cooked up, and salted. They were known as little fried things—aka *fritos*. Doolin, who had a history of health problems, didn't eat salt or fried food, but he saw the line of people and their reactions after tasting the corn chips. His eyes opened wide as he saw what others had missed: an inexpensive, easy to make snack that could be manufactured and would take off like wildfire with the public.

After buying the patent, Doolin went home and refined the recipe. He loved to experiment and installed kitchens like secret laboratories everywhere he lived and worked. In one such kitchen he also invented the Cheeto. In my research, I was happy to learn that Doolin always had his kids and other family members serve as his original tasters and recipe developers (something I'd always done).

C. E. Doolin originally saw Fritos as a garnish or small side dish, not as a main attraction meant to be eaten in large quantities. Nevertheless, he promoted homestyle recipes that made a meal out of Fritos and printed them on the back of the packaging. You may have heard of Frito Pie (slice open a bag of Fritos, heat up some canned chili and put a heap of it on the chips, then take a spoon and eat it out of the package). But have you heard of no-cook Fritos Chocolate Crunchies? How about Fritos Squash Casserole?

I loved checking out the original designs of the early Fritos and Cheetos packaging. On the operational end of things, Doolin adapted elements of Henry Ford's assembly line for producing the chips—on a scale that was not being done at the time. Then Doolin did something no other brand could have conceived of doing and launched a restaurant at Disneyland, calling it Casa de Fritos. You could not get more American-as-apple-pie than being associated with the happiest place on earth.

Now, unlike Fritos, which had come up from the streets, potato chips got their start in fine cuisine—most likely in French cooking of the 1800s. As the story goes, the first time a reference to potato chips showed up in the United States was in 1853 at an exclusive restaurant in Saratoga Springs, New York. The chef was annoyed when a demanding customer (some said Cornelius Vanderbilt) sent back his French-fried potatoes and said they weren't crisp enough. Irritated, the chef then whipped up a batch of super thin, crunchy potato chips, never expecting them to be a hit. Pretty soon Saratoga Chips, as they became known, had put the restaurant on the map.

The rage took off and small companies around the country developed their own potato chip brands. One such company was started in the 1930s by Herman W. Lay of Nashville, Tennessee, a snack food and beverage distributor. Wanting to be different from all the competition, he set the ambitious goal of creating a *national* chip brand—something that did not exist at the time.

Herman Lay purchased existing companies with factories

that were not doing well and turned their businesses around, making his company—Lay's—one of the biggest in the Southeast. Lay also famously cared about his workers and believed that the key to his success had come from his interest in people and seeing others succeed.

In 1961, a merger between the Frito Company of Dallas and Lay's, both household names, became official, and a powerhouse was born. C. E. Doolin passed away before the merger was complete, but Herman Lay—who became board chairman of the newly formed Frito-Lay—honored both companies by achieving his dream of creating the first national snack food brand. Lay's next dream was even bigger—to go international.

Enter Donald M. Kendall, the head of Pepsi-Cola, an executive I would later learn a lot from. In 1965, when Herman Lay negotiated a merger between Frito-Lay and Pepsi, Kendall became cofounder (with Herman Lay) of the newly formed PepsiCo and was made its president and CEO. Don Kendall had already turned Pepsi's fortunes around after starting at the bottom of the Pepsi food chain as a syrup salesman. Within ten years he was an executive leading its international division. While Coca-Cola was the top-selling American cola in much of Europe, Kendall masterminded a strategy to introduce Pepsi behind the Iron Curtain—beating Coke in the process. Don Kendall inspired me incredibly as someone who had come up from an entry level and made it to the very top—with a tough but visionary style all his own.

By learning the brand histories of Frito-Lay, Pepsi, and

PepsiCo, I also was able to study the who's who of the corporation. Getting to know them and their contributions, more than anything, helped me to take a giant step toward learning to think like an executive. At the least, I learned not to be intimidated while approaching these higher-ups when I thought I had something of interest to them. That's one common denominator for how the best executives think—they rarely want to pass up a discovery that can be profitable.

In addition to getting to know Don Kendall, who remained fully in action on the board as our corporate founder and CEO of PepsiCo (based in New York), I was in touch with his second-in-command, Wayne Calloway (the CEO of Pepsi-Cola, who was heading up Frito-Lay out of Dallas and who would succeed Don as CEO of PepsiCo in 1986). Wayne—who never lost his North Carolina drawl—was a devout church-goer who loved self-help books and riding his Harley, and always seemed open to fresh ideas.

From the very first time I sent samples of a possible innovation (oversized chips good for dipping) to Don Kendall and Wayne Calloway, they had both enthusiastically encouraged me to send them innovative ideas anytime. From studying the ways that executives think, I took that to mean they weren't just being nice. They were genuinely interested and appreciative. Whenever I did send something, I was careful to make it worth their while. Like the time when I'd seen kids in my neighborhood get seasoning packets of lime and chili from the ice-cream truck. At the swap meet, I picked up a few packets for a dime apiece and sent them off to Wayne Calloway. Next thing I knew, everyone at headquarters was talking about the next big flavor trend—yes, you guessed it—lime and chili.

A short while later, I received a letter thanking me for excellence in innovation from Wayne Calloway, along with an enclosed stock certificate. That made me the first frontline nonexecutive to receive stock—one share. His gesture revealed another aspect of how to think like an executive: taking the time to motivate employees.

Don Kendall, Wayne Calloway, and, later, Roger Enrico (Calloway's brilliant successor, who became CEO of Pepsi-Cola at the age of thirty-seven, and then at forty-four was asked to come over to lead Frito-Lay) embodied for me the two traits I eventually identified as key to executive leadership: *excellence* and *competence.*

The simplest way to describe the difference, the way I see it, is that excellence is about being the best that you can be, whereas competence or technical competence is you being the best at something. A little etymology might shed more light on these two traits.

Excellence derives from the Latin *excellentia*: "superiority, greatness, distinction," from *ex*, "out from," plus *cellere*, "rise high, tower," related to *celsus*, "high, lofty, great."* To be the best you, then, is to be willing to rise up to lofty, spiritual heights. Striving for excellence or motivating others toward excellence can be more of a spiritual quest, a drive that comes from the heart with a spirit of excellence.

---

*Online Etymology Dictionary, s.v. "excellence (n.)," www.etymonline .com/word/excellence.

Competence comes from the French and Latin and refers to "sufficiency for living at ease" and "adequate range of capacity or ability."* Technical competence, as a trait that's important for executive leadership, also refers to being fluent with systems—how they work and what to do when they break down. Competence, a quality of being good *at* something, can be seen as more intellectual than emotional. When it comes to making decisions, competence would lead an executive to make a more pragmatic, strategic decision.

I was always curious to hear directly from executives about what they value in employees. One of my mentors later on in my journey used to commend me for having technical competence. For him, brand history was important, sales and marketing were obviously important, but the most important emphasis for him was—*you have to know your product.* Companies sell products or services so, clearly, if you want to think like an executive, it behooves you to get to know your product inside and out.

The best decision makers at the executive level think with both their head and their heart. When I ascended to executive status and had to make decisions about offers, I used head and heart to evaluate the deal—would this be good for my people and provide opportunities for them to achieve excellence and/or did it make sense in terms of technical competence and the company's bottom line?

By doing my homework—learning from higher-ups about

Online Etymology Dictionary, s.v. "competence (*n.*)," www.etymonline .com/word/competence.

how they reached decisions—I got into the habit of practicing being the future me—in my mind. This was not a practice I made up on my own but was something I'd learned from role models and mentors who'd helped me stretch and grow— sometimes without even knowing they were helping.

WE'VE PROBABLY ALL SEEN THE IMAGE OF SUCCESS IN CORPORATE America and elsewhere as a ladder to be climbed—rung by rung, step by step. Yet there are many of us—maybe not from mainstream business backgrounds—who see it differently. For us, it's not as straightforward as a ladder that leads you vertically up and up. My view is that it's more like rock climbing. You might take one step up but then you have to reach to the side horizontally and find a different footing. You're constantly reaching and stretching as you climb the rocks, small and large, to success. Sometimes it may feel as if you're out there alone with sheer rock walls to scale and boulders that block your way up. Most of the time, though, you can be aided by the examples of others who have come before you or even some who are willing to give you some pointers.

You can call that person your Sherpa, your guide, your role model, or, perhaps, your mentor. It's not necessary to give someone an official title in order to learn from them everything you need to know about moving up in the world. Interestingly enough, many of the most successful executives I've ever met believed in the importance of mentoring—just as they had been mentored at some point.

At Frito-Lay, many of the managers would tolerate me, but they didn't always appreciate me. I was forever breaking ranks, stepping onto their turf, acting like an owner, and thinking like an executive. They wore expressions that clearly said, "Who do you think you are?" They were constantly reminding me that they weren't paying me for my personal striving for excellence and competence.

There was one exception, more than anyone else in my early years, who taught me how to think, dress, speak, and carry myself like an executive. A production manager, Julius C. McGee was one of the boldest, most charismatic yet most understated and even humblest individuals I have ever met. African American and born in the 1940s, Julius was from a small town in Oklahoma and had been forced to deal with extreme discrimination growing up. He had been shot at, spat on, called the worst names, and refused college admission even though he was brilliant. More than anything, he taught me how to rise above the haters, never to let discrimination make me bitter or a victim. He explained that his choice to resist the bitterness was his way of winning and of being free to be Julius C. McGee.

Julius commanded your respect the minute he walked into a room because (a) he was respectful, (b) he had a cool walk, and (c) he'd arrive at work in his long black leather coat—like a movie detective. Inspired, I began to cultivate my own look with the few things I could afford at Goodwill. In that period, managers and floor workers were expected to dress differently from each other. Managers had dress khakis and long-sleeved button-down dress shirts. Floor workers had blue work uniforms—like gas station attendants. When I decided to start wearing khakis and a dress shirt, I got stares from other managers.

A few would ask, "What do you think you're doing?"

I answered, "Getting ready for the future."

Everyone was up in arms until some of the other frontline workers started dressing like managers too. About a year later, the dress code was changed.

Julius should have been a vice president, but as a nonconformist and a minority in that era, he didn't fit the profile. Still, he thought like an executive—and was a math wizard who was the main reason I gained technical competence. He also pushed me to ask for promotions and raises.

"Richard," he would always say, "you are a superstar, don't sell yourself for a steak dinner."

Years later I read the story of how Odysseus, king of Ithaca, before departing for the Trojan War, asked a friend to look after his son in case he didn't return. That friend promised, "I will teach and raise him as my own son." The friend's name was Mentor—which is where the word comes from. Mentoring—the process of investing one's time, energy, and know-how in the development of someone else—is much like parenting and much to be admired.

I've always said that my first nine years of working at Frito-Lay was the equivalent of getting my GED plus a college degree and some grad school. My experience with Julius

and the head of operations at the plant—who kept their doors
open whenever I had questions—taught me that moving up
in the corporate structure was something I didn't have to figure out all on my own.

Over the years, thanks to these early experiences, I sought
out mentors and role models without the need to apologize
or ask for permission. Some of them didn't know they were
mentoring me. The process was much more collegial. True, I
was a janitor and they were often directors, vice presidents,
even, as later events would prove, CEOs.

There are a handful of strategies you can always employ
when you decide to practice the future you and learn to think
like an executive by seeking advice from someone who can
help you climb your mountain.

* If you know you might get the chance to meet a potential
  mentor or have the ear of someone whose advice you'd like,
  do your homework about their track record and accomplishments. Have a couple of questions ready that are not
  only specific to your interest but may also make that person
  feel comfortable talking about themselves. Who doesn't
  like talking about themselves?
* If you have someone in mind who might be a terrific mentor but don't want to come across as taking up too much of
  their time, you don't have to use that word. You can offer to
  buy coffee, and maybe the two of you can have an "informa-
  tional." If you've done your homework, you'll be able to ask
  questions related to their work. Thinking like an executive,

prepare for that meeting with a spirit of excellence—to be the best you that you can. Also be ready to emphasize your competence—something that you are excellent at.

* Don't wait for your employer (or prospective employer if you are on a job hunt) to bring up the subject of your promotion, a raise, or a compensation package. Many of us get nervous asking for what we need and think we could be replaced or fired for asking for what we want. Be yourself, be direct, and put it on the table. Let the other person make the offer if possible. Usually, they'll lowball the offer and that's your floor. Now find out what the ceiling is.

* Know that it's okay to be competitive. When you look around your place of work and notice a fellow employee who is at a higher rank than you, it's okay to want to be in their spot and learn from their technical competence and the ways they excel at certain things. That's how they can become your mentor without even knowing it.

The art of practicing the future you can be fun, creative, and liberating. You may not be at the executive level yet, but as you take on the attributes and mind-set of someone who is highly valued by the company, you carry yourself with a certain energy and poise that you may never have had before. The beautiful thing that can happen next is that as you think like an executive, you'll have an inside scoop on the kinds of problem-solving solutions and innovations that executives will want to know about. You will develop a sixth sense about ideas that really are hot and those that are not.

4

The Best Ideas Are Served Hot

ey, I had a billion-dollar brainstorm but after I told a friend, he stole the idea and ran with it!" a gentleman who tried to make it in the tech world once confided to me.

Ideas are never stolen. This may sound harsh, but it's the truth. We either act on our ideas or we don't. By acting on an idea, I mean that you invest your own time in it by researching, developing, and promoting its reality. That way, you're turning it into a thing of value that has your name on it. You're also safeguarding it from having anyone come along, borrow your concept to make it their own, and hijack your destiny. If you want to avoid that fate, my advice is to hold your ideas—like your cards—close.

More important, though, is to remember that if you don't act fast, you run the risk of having the idea go stale.

The point is—when you've got something good cooking, don't forget that the best ideas are served hot. So set that table.

"GOT A MINUTE?" I CAN REMEMBER ASKING JULIUS ONE DAY AS I STOOD in the open doorway of his office. He was getting ready to go home, dressed in his long black leather coat, and I didn't want to make him late.

He waved me in, asking what seemed to be so urgent. When I showed him my notebook and the notes I'd been keeping, he seemed pleased at the trouble he knew I was about to cause. He also knew it was trouble that could have a major impact on improving the company's bottom line.

In my role as a janitor, after learning how to work the line and getting hired for extra hours when shift workers didn't show, I'd been promoted to the general utility squad—which meant I knew every square inch of the facility. There was not one single piece of equipment that I hadn't cleaned or didn't know what it was and how it worked. What I had uncovered was something that nobody else seemed to have noticed or prioritized: *waste*.

When you grow up in a family of eleven kids—eating cafeteria style with other farm laborers and their families—you learn to keep an eye out for any morsel of extra food that would go to waste if you didn't claim it. On the one hand, I could appreciate the strict guidelines for quality control that

Frito-Lay enforced. On the other hand, it made no sense to me that we were losing perfectly good product because of human error or that raw materials, supplies, and equipment parts were being carelessly thrown out.

Being from the ghetto and maybe because I'd watched my father fix anything and make it new again, I would always look at waste and take it personally. Certainly, that's how I felt after starting to measure how much food, labor, supplies, and profit were literally being thrown out every day at Frito-Lay. Unnecessarily.

There were a few culprits that I could identify. Mainly, there were no universal practices in every plant that every employee had to follow. It was just assumed that the porters would come and get rid of whatever needed to be thrown away. In the 1960s and '70s, for the first time there were awareness campaigns and public service announcements about littering. Those were the days when you'd see people throwing trash out of their car windows without any thought of taking care of public spaces. We didn't have a littering problem inside the factory, of course, but the average worker hadn't been trained to be mindful of using everything inside containers of ingredients before throwing them away. In almost every shift, extra product that didn't get properly packaged and boxed would end up being carted off. This happened a lot after the line backed up.

In those three stages of production—processing, packaging, and shipping—the critical stage was the packaging. First of all, there were multiple sizes of bags to be packed into boxes, which were then laid on the pallets to be sent to a warehouse for shipping. If there was a delay and only ten bags got sealed in time to make it into a box meant for twelve, that unfinished box would have to wait to be placed on a pallet. The product went into bags that hung from a machine; the bags would then get sealed, pulled from the assembly line, and dropped into the box. There was no mechanism to get the right number of bags into a box when the line was moving too fast or too slow. Sometimes the person who ran the line would fix it manually but not always, which would slow down the process considerably and result in a loss of hundreds of dollars or more per day. So the challenge I gave myself was to figure out what could be done when, say, a couple of the unfilled bags would fall off the line or not be pulled in time. If you could keep the line moving without errors, you could save time and money.

As I learned, the machine operator who cut the bags could make or break a shift; cutters had to make sure they could cut twenty bags per minute, flawlessly. For smaller bags they could do many times that amount. The focus was to fill a certain weight of chips into the same size bags systematically—to cut/fold, fill, and seal the bags. When there was a delay of any type, we'd wind up with a situation known as skipping bags, because you could have a couple of empties here and there that the product would miss.

Skipped bags were not a problem for the operators, because the assembly line would slow down—into a stroll rather than a sprint. They even liked it. Nonetheless, it was waste, and because I was already thinking like an executive and acting like an owner, I believed someone up the chain of command should know about the problem and a simple checklist I created for preventing waste. Before mentioning my checklist to anyone, I wanted to offer modifications that would help, depending on which line was being run.

During my breaks, after hours, and on weekends, I asked questions of Julius and others, scouted around, and kept notes about where most of the waste was happening. The least of the waste on the lines I noted was in the space where we made Cheetos, interestingly enough—one of the hardest chips to make but the easiest chips for bagging. All because of bulk density—the physics of what something weighs versus the space it occupies.

Cheetos and Fritos are heavy chips. They're like rocks, so when they fall into a bag, they really drop right into place, without a hitch. The bulk density of potato chips, especially, and tortilla chips are the opposite. They're bigger but lighter, leading to the potential for breakage and other concerns during bagging. The lighter, bigger chips sort of float on their way down, and that requires the operator to work more meticulously to make sure bags are full.

By the way, the beautiful thing about a Cheeto is that it is actually popped into existence. At Frito-Lay the processing of certain chips, such as Cheetos, was referred to as *extruded*—cornmeal and water forced through a tube, like squeezing toothpaste out, then shot into a die with a blade that cuts it into its miniature Cheeto shape, still raw and mushy until it gets fried. As it hits the oil in the fryer, it *pops* itself into a preseasoned puff of a chip—tasteless but crunchy and ready for the wet application of cheese and seasoning known as slurry.

As I did my analysis of where the company was losing money by wasting supplies, I went on a fact-finding mission to seek out the most minute details. Little did I know that understanding these problems inside and out was going to come in very handy later on with bigger ideas. By becoming such a self-taught expert in how, for example, Cheetos came into being compared with Tostitos, I could measure how many materials were needed for each shift for optimal production and how much was going to waste—corn, oil, seasoning, and so on.

Julius looked over my notes and the checklist I'd created for how to solve the problem of wasteful practices and just smiled. Then, as if I had been the batboy watching the game and he was telling me to go on up to the plate and take my swing at the ball, he handed the notes back to me and said, "What are you waiting for?"

He meant that it was up to me, still known to all as the janitor, to reach out to someone up the chain of command to communicate my innovative approach to saving the company money. Julius knew the kind of racism and resistance I'd face. As an African American who had overcome the same barriers, and worse, he knew there would be some who wouldn't want to hear me out. Yes, he could have intervened as a go-between, but he would never have run the risk of appearing to take credit for my insights. As a leader, he had that kind of integrity. He knew, long before I saw it, that this was an opportunity I'd created for myself that would let me reach up to one of those higher rocks I'd been climbing toward.

Whenever I'm asked how to have a hot idea that should be

acted on right away, I'm fast to point out that the most profitable or impactful ideas often come about in order to solve a pressing problem. From the invention of the wheel to the electric wiring of the first light bulb, almost every technological leap into the future we now can't live without began when someone scratched their head and said—*Hmm, something's not working as well as it could. What else could we do?*

If you ask most leaders, visionaries, creators, and entrepreneurs the secret to their hottest ideas, they will tell you that they were looking for a new or better way to fix an existing problem or a significant void in the marketplace.

Your concern may not be a problem that others recognize as urgent. However, once you manage to communicate the problem and show how much your solution is needed, ladies and gentlemen, you've got a hot idea!

Now I had a new problem, though. How was I going to communicate to someone higher up the chain? And how could I do it quickly enough to take advantage of information that was hot off the press? My sense of urgency came from the fact that from the time of the founder, C. E. Doolin, the Frito-Lay philosophy was to continually implement innovative best practices. If anyone found out that I was developing a solution that might go over big with HQ, they could come along and take credit for it in a heartbeat. That was one issue. My other concern was that if I didn't go all out right away, the project ran the risk of my feeling either overwhelmed by the ambition of it or insecure that I couldn't communicate the problem satisfactorily.

So I knew that time was of the essence. Still, I had to mull over the question I'm often asked about how we find the right opening to put ourselves (or our ideas) in front of the right person at the right time.

The answer lies—in part—in understanding the true meaning of opportunity.

Like a lot of words that have traveled to the English language over many miles and over long periods of time, the word *opportunity* came about as a hybrid of other words. The Latin term *opportunitas* is composed of two other terms: *ob*, meaning "toward," and *portus*, meaning "port." In the field of navigation, sailors used the phrase *ob portus* to describe the best combination of wind, current, and tide for sailing *toward port*.* It wasn't enough for sailors to know the weather conditions. Those would mean little without the ability to create an opportunity by steering toward a clear destination.

In the olden days, the ship captain had to wait until the flood tides came in so the oceangoing vessel could get close to the shore. Knowing the right time to return to port (or to launch out) required him to keenly observe the wind, current, and tide. If he didn't steer the ship at the right moment, the opportunity to get back to port would be missed.

A hot idea—one that will solve a problem or engage an audience—can be made much hotter by seizing an opportunity that may not come again. For example, even though I didn't know it, PepsiCo was already looking for ways to become more environmentally responsible and reduce waste.

**Online Etymology Dictionary*, s.v. "opportunity (*n*.)," www.etymonline .com/word/opportunity.

Here I was with a solution. If I hadn't been eager to move on it, somebody else was going to, and soon.

Opportunities aren't handed to us. We create our own opportunities just as we sail our own ships.

That is, in fact, what I was able to do. But first I had to learn how to use a computer.

IN THE MID-1980S, AS FRITO-LAY MOVED QUICKLY TO MODERNIZE ITS office technology, most of the midlevel managers had begun to have access to desktop computers. For anyone else who might need to run a report or send a memo, there were a couple of extra computers that could be accessed.

On my breaks and after hours, I'd sit and stare at the screen, trying to figure out how to navigate a completely foreign dimension. Managers would do double takes as they'd walk by, wanting to know why the janitor was taking up company time and one of the few spare computers. "Make sure you clock out," they'd all say, adding, "We're not paying you to learn the computer." Or: "Do what we pay you to do."

One night as I sat there with a dictionary, trying to type up my letter and a report, one of the few female managers, Gina, walked by, and saw me struggling.

"I'm off the clock," I said before she could say anything.

Gina wasn't concerned. When I explained that this was a letter and a report that I wanted to give to our plant manager or maybe someone at headquarters, she was impressed. Just before leaving for the night, she said, "You know, Richard, you don't need a dictionary."

"Well, I'm not the best speller," I admitted. If only she knew!

Gina laughed and then told me about spell-check. After that, she proceeded to show me the fundamentals of word processing. When she saw how ambitiously I'd envisioned the report, she became invested in my success. Over the next several days, Gina managed to teach me all she knew about the computer—how to create graphs, charts, and crazy multicolored graphics. My report suddenly looked like it had been developed by a pro.

At times, I look back at that moment and wonder what might have happened if one of the testier, more critical bosses had happened by. Gina showing up at the right place at just the right time was *a lesson in trusting that people will come into your life to help you do the things you are destined to do.*

Now, however, the next moves were on me.

In the command and control system of that time, going above the heads of your immediate bosses was seen as outright insubordination. Could I be fired? Probably not. But I could be demoted, resented, and ostracized. My checklist for ending waste did require more work from the operators and managers. By this point, I was on my way to making nine dollars an hour, still not enough to make ends meet. So was it worth the risk to my future livelihood to try to save money for the company?

Well, why overthink it? My goal was to identify a problem and offer a solution. I quietly went to see the plant manager and handed him the report.

To this day, I don't know how he reacted initially. I do know that he couldn't just throw away the report. After all, I was the janitor. If it ended up in the trash, I'd know it!

A short time later, all employees were notified that the Rancho Cucamonga plant would be adopting a series of new practices aimed at stopping waste throughout our facility. Soon those same practices were adopted in every Frito-Lay plant in the country and beyond. Crediting me, our plant manager had decided the ideas were worthy—why not send them on to the top executives of our company?

In an instance of excellent, opportune conditions for my waste-busting program, the vice president of Frito-Lay was then the visionary, charismatic Albert Carey. It turned out that Al Carey was already a champion of innovative practices that would help our company become more environmentally conscious. Preventing waste and litter, recycling reusable materials, becoming an industry-wide leader, saving money—these were concerns already on his radar. Timing, clearly, made all the difference for my proposal.

The changes went into effect almost immediately. They would go on to save the company many millions over the years to come. After being acknowledged as employee of the month, I was given a small raise. It didn't bother me so much that I wasn't given a ticker-tape parade or a big promotion. Even if no one says a word, sometimes the reward for a great idea is that you will know your capability. You are just warming up for something bigger.

Predictably, some of the managers were angry that I'd overstepped my position. There were no Mexican American managers at the time, and some of their comments were vaguely racist, such as, "We appreciate the effort, Montañez, but you should leave programs like this to the college graduates." Then there was the response to that comment, spoken to someone else in front of me: "This guy thinks he's a VP and doesn't even know how to speak right." A couple of the managers asked if I had lifted the ideas from somewhere else. One manager complimented my work but then added it was good that I wasn't "the lazy kind." Unfortunately, those stereotypical remarks about being illiterate, uneducated, lazy, and a thief were far too common.

Some managers and coworkers were proud and gave me props—with appreciation for the improved guidelines. Many didn't know the changes had even come from my suggestions.

An interesting experience happened about a year after my report created waves at the corporation. It taught me a lesson I have used ever since about how opportunities come our way. We're all told that success can depend on "who you know." What I learned is that it's less about who you know and more about who knows you. Al Carey had never met me, and we had never had any written interactions, which was not unusual, but he knew of me from my report on waste. One day at the plant, everyone was buzzing about how he was coming to Rancho Cucamonga—unheard of for a vice president.

But that was Al Carey, an executive who cared about getting to meet and know as many employees as he could. The directors and managers would be having lunch with him, but there were no planned events for any of the frontline workers to meet him.

By chance, on the appointed day of his arrival, I was nearby when he walked into the main entrance, surrounded by upper-level managers, and was about to start his official tour of our plant. There seemed to be a pause in the progress of the tour—an opening to go over and introduce myself. This was sacrilege, against all the rules of corporate command and control. But the ghetto came out in me. In my day, I had seen grown men go after each other with knives. This was nuthin'!

As I walked up, several managers turned multiple shades of green.

"Mr. Carey," I began, my arm outstretched. "We haven't met. I'm Richard Montañez, part of the general utility crew. . . ." Before I could finish, he took my hand and shook it vigorously.

"Of course! Nice to meet you in person, Richard." He congratulated me on the success of the program.

When I mentioned that I'd been tinkering with other projects, he handed me his card with his direct number, making me promise to call him whenever I had anything to run by him.

And indeed I would—when not too much later I had my next truly hot idea.

IN THE START-UP WORLD, AND TO MANY EXPERTS WHO TRACK THE breakthroughs of entrepreneurs and innovators, the conventional wisdom is that you might have only one or two big ideas in you. I don't agree. I believe each of us has the potential to be a wellspring of ideas. Whether or not they give us our big breaks or take us *ob portus*—toward port—is up to our expertise and our choice to be the captains of our own ships.

You and your confidence will *pop* when the mind-set of ownership meets the knowledge gained by paying close attention to the way business is run—for weeks, months, and years. Your ability to create opportunities and take advantage of timing are always dependent on how you harness patience as an asset on your journey, but also how you learn to move quickly when you have a hot, timely, or needed idea.

What if you don't have that confidence just yet? What if you're not sure you can come up with something that's new or relevant? Those are questions I hear often. Many of us can relate to feeling that way. The remedy, as we've seen, is to shift our mind-set to think like executives and act like owners by improving the conditions for creating ideas and opportunities. Give some of these strategies a try:

1. *Be a problem solver.* Spend a day or two taking stock of your current work setting and asking yourself how you would like to see it improve. Pay attention, for example, to

how certain duties are being duplicated. Is there a way you can propose to streamline those efforts? Many businesses right now spend way too much time and resources with employees often doing the same job or even double work—printing out or mailing forms than can easily be sent electronically. If you see room for improvement in your industry, what ideas do you have to solve those problems that make sense to you? Then start to envision how the environment will improve with those changes. The shift in thinking is that instead of feeling like you are just a cog in the wheel, you begin to see the value of your contribution.

2. *Itemize your earlier ideas.* As children, many of us have exciting ideas about what we want to be and do when we grow up. Our imaginations aren't limited yet by cold reality. When you go back to the past and recall your ambitious and fun ideas, you are engaging the opportunist in yourself—never a bad thing. Maybe it was how you made a lot of money with a side hustle as a teenager, or you came up with a creative concept for a school project or acted on ideas to redecorate and transform your living space. You could have had a wild idea that didn't work because it wasn't the right time, or you didn't know how to pitch it. But it's proof that you are on the right track for having a hotter idea the next time.

3. *Turn your lemons into lemon meringue pie.* Notice I didn't say lemonade! I'm saying that the most winning ideas are often original or quirky concepts that come to you in the midst of hungry times. At Frito-Lay, a machine

that cut chips into smaller pieces once broke down. The product was about to get trashed when I looked at one of the chips and saw something that gave me an idea—abnormally big chips would be great for better dipping. So I put a big chip in a bag and sent it off to HQ to our corporate founder and also sent a sample to the CEO of our parent corporation. Intrigued, they sent my samples to the research and development team, which took over and tried to re-create it and turn that mistake into a new product that was a hit. What an eye-opener! The lesson is that if you look at mistakes and mishaps as opportunities to learn from, or let them reveal a better way to avoid errors next time, you're creating an opportunity to become known as an idea person.

4. *Embrace your purpose.* Where you are today may not be where you'd like to be tomorrow or next week, but if you challenge yourself to see the purpose of where you've landed, you'll be more inclined to see that the seeds of opportunity are being planted by all that you're learning. You may not have a CEO or higher-up who encourages all employees to develop and contribute ideas for the company's bottom line. Still, we really are living in a "we're all in this together" time when the next huge idea might be a life-saving one or could make someone's job easier who is an essential worker or is working on the front lines of fighting a pandemic. You may not be a doctor who can develop a treatment or a vaccine, but even in challenging times there can be opportunities to look for ideas for being of service to others.

There are two other practices I strongly suggest for boosting your idea-development skills. They come from my experiences that helped me feel safe, create opportunities, and have fun in the process: (a) Create an idea brainstorming circle; and (b) start small. It's important that the people you invite into your brainstorming circle are individuals you trust, like your close family members and colleagues; it's helpful to know in advance that if anything worthwhile comes from your efforts, everyone will share in the opportunity. Make it safe for anyone to float ideas that might not have any merit, but at least you can get feedback when something sounds interesting. My family was my brainstorming circle, and we used to play with different ideas for side hustles or product inventions and improvements. I'd get the family together and give out ten M&M's to everyone and we'd each get a paper cup we'd use for developing new ideas. The rule was that if you had a good idea, you'd get another M&M. If you were overly negative about someone's idea, then you'd have to put an M&M back. If I said, "Well, I'm going to create a cup without a base," and one of the kids said, "That's a bad idea!" they'd have to give up an M&M. If one of the kids proposed to put air-conditioning in the cup, I'd nod and say, "That's original," and that kid would get an M&M. It was safe and fun, not to mention tasty.

When you do decide to act on an idea, it can serve you well to start small because you're practicing the steps necessary for getting the idea into the world. Go as small as possible. Maybe you see a product or article that could be of interest to a boss or someone who could sign on to your own ideas down the road—send that on to them. You'll be earning a reputation as someone with good instincts who's paying attention to trends in the news and in the marketplace. Plus, you'll be gaining the experience and belief in yourself that are needed when it's time to act on something bigger.

What happens when you think you've really got something good—when you think it's time to move fast?

There are three main considerations that you can use to test whether your revelation of an idea is hot, whether the timing is opportune or not, or whether you might need to go back to the drawing board. Let's look at those three considerations and at some of the different industries where ideas gain traction. First, ask some of these questions to gauge your heat:

1. *Would someone else want to steal this idea?* Take the example of the nurse working in ICU settings with stroke patients and others unable to speak who created a set of drawings that became a communication picture board. For example, a patient could point to where it hurt on their body or a picture of what pain level they were feeling. A life-and-death idea! It was stealable for sure! She went home, developed a prototype, and then invested her own money into producing the boards and sold them to her bosses at the hospital.

2. *Is there an opportunity in terms of timing or heightened interest that will add appeal to your idea?* A shoe store clerk was always hearing complaints from teen customers about how difficult it was to keep their sneakers looking clean, so when he heard of a small local company that had an amazing spray-on solution for cleaning and protecting all kinds

of materials, he tested the solution on his own sneakers and saw that it cleaned them up like magic. He worked out a deal with the little company and they partnered on what he saw as a side hustle. At a time when the economy was down and kids were being told they could only buy one pair of sneakers rather than three, he pounced on the opportunity to sell a product that would keep that one pair looking new all the time. He started selling it at swap meets, and just at a moment when his idea could have been stolen, he heard of a company that distributed an array of cleaning and protective products, and sold his business to that distributor—making a big profit for himself and the owners of the company that had invented the solution.

3. *Can you create a demo or prototype quickly and inexpensively?* Right before the pandemic closed down so many businesses, an office manager at a large financial institution had been tinkering with a proposal to hold meetings virtually. As soon as the shutdown happened, she was able to revise her proposal and connect to a videoconferencing operation that helped her demonstrate her idea to her bosses, who wisely endorsed her idea and didn't miss any employee downtime as a result.

Having the ability to act on an idea that's timely is a major asset. It's also good to take ideas that aren't so hot or urgent and try to develop them as if they were. You're just warming up and practicing your idea-developing skills. That's what happened in my case. Unconsciously, by starting out with smaller ideas, I had been setting the stage for those bigger ideas that I had been anticipating and praying would be revealed to me.

When you have a compelling product or concept or innovative approach, you never have to ask for permission to act on it—just do it already. Don't be discouraged by obstacles or critics. Doors will open. The right people will come through to point you toward your destiny.

When a hot idea put into action fails, it is not your failure, by the way. It's a sign from the universe that you've learned to act on your own ideas. So keep at it. There were plenty of ideas that I tried that went nowhere. The program I created for ending waste didn't make me rich, but it gained me enough respect that when my bosses were thinking of developing new training manuals for different equipment, they asked me to take the lead. Can you believe it? Then they asked me to train frontline workers and operators on new procedures, equipment, and protocols. I was still the janitor who did a few other things not in my job description. My efforts to master the computer in order to write up that first report also paid many dividends. Running with an idea in a timely manner had given me a confidence and a belief that I was very close to a signature revelation. The takeaway was that I could do even more—once I found that right idea that would be even bigger, even hotter.

There is another critical key in gaining traction for your revelations that I wish had been explained to me earlier on. That's next.

5

Don't Be Afraid to Look Ridiculous

(Shh! Because Greatness Often Comes in Ridiculous Forms!)

Did you know that the most famous leaders, entrepreneurs, innovators, and inventors in the world had to first find the courage to appear ridiculous before they achieved success?

This is one of the best-kept secrets to greatness. None of the top MBA programs in the country mention it, at least not in my experience from having lectured at most of them. Even so, I promise you, greatness often comes in ridiculous forms. It took me years to realize how to harness the energy of ridiculousness, even though I started learning about it at a very young age.

ON THE FIRST DAY OF THE THIRD GRADE, I LEARNED THAT THE SEATING arrangements during lunchtime had changed. Instead of sitting with our minority group, I had to find places at other tables where I could squeeze in. Previously, my brown-skinned friends and I had remained segregated from the other students, eating our lunches off in our own huddle, at a distance. In what felt like the beginning of a horror movie, it hit me that I was about to walk into the trap of being ridiculed worse than in a knife fight.

Looking around at the tables with all the white kids opening up their lunch in unison, I could have sworn that everyone had the same lunch—bologna on white bread and a cupcake. The terror on my face must have drawn everyone's attention. I had yet to take my lunch out of the bag, and I knew that it definitely was not going to be a bologna sandwich.

In a nightmare scenario, as if time stood still, from my point of view every single person at every lunch table turned their heads in slow motion to stare at me as I took out my lunch. Their faces registered the fact that this was clearly the most ridiculous, foreign sight any of them had ever seen. Yes, for those of you who may have guessed, you are right. My lunch was a burrito.

Like a flying saucer had just dropped an alien shape from outer space into my lunch bag, the sight of my burrito made the other third-graders all laugh and point at me uproariously. Then they went back to their bologna. I was *mortified*. Hungry as I was, I felt too ridiculous and ashamed to eat. Slowly and casually, I slid the burrito back into my lunch sack. My stomach groaned, but it was not as bad as the possibility that I could be mocked again.

In hindsight, I can understand that this was the 1960s, and there were almost no Taco Bells or Del Tacos or prominent Mexican restaurants, or even lone vendors around. Historically speaking, it turns out that it was not a taco stand that introduced the burrito to the Inland Empire—it was my mom and me!

That day when I went home, I told her about the embarrassment and handed her the burrito. "Tomorrow," I begged, "pack me a bologna sandwich and a cupcake like all the other kids!"

"No, *mijo*," she refused, holding my uneaten lunch, "this is who you are."

I looked back at her helplessly.

"You know," she said, "I have a better idea."

Marketing genius that my mother was, the next day she handed me my lunch—only this time the bag had not one but two burritos in it. She explained, "Here is one burrito for you and one to make a friend with."

Under my breath, I must have muttered something like "That's ridiculous," but I had to try *something*. Otherwise I would starve.

That Thursday, I had no choice but to get past my fear of looking foolish and find a friend who wanted to try a burrito.

To my shock, it was easy! Who knew that at least one kid was bored with having the same lunch day after day?

Next thing I knew, everything had changed and I became a young entrepreneur. From Wednesday when I had the one ridiculous burrito, to Thursday when my mother gave me two burritos, I arrived at school on Friday with two bags full of burritos to sell for twenty-five cents apiece. And sold out! What was once ridiculous became delicious. Now I was in business. Or I should say, Mama and I were.

Lesson learned. Hunger could be an antidote to fear, and the hunger of other kids to taste something new and different could lead to a reward. All I had needed to risk was the fleeting sting of looking ridiculous.

What had just happened? Well, at the age of eight, I'd been given my first revelation, which led to a revolution. The truth that was revealed to me (by me!) was that fitting in was overrated. As much as you want to fit in with the prevailing system, you have to realize that you are too flamin' hot to be average, to fit in. You were never created to play it safe and not risk being different or even ridiculous. You were created to shine, to be special, to stand out.

Of course, much of the working world doesn't understand the value of having employees or executives come up with ridiculous products or marketing ideas. That's unfortunate because companies that profit from innovation should want to create environments where employees feel safe sounding ridiculous while thinking outside the box. Think of all the successful entrepreneurial ventures that emerged when developers had the courage to suggest highfalutin ideas that were funny or outrageous or silly. No one in the world needed a pet rock. But somebody came up with the concept, the toy industry decided to get behind it, and the fad earned millions of dollars. The creators of Facebook didn't intend to compete with Myspace; they just wanted to create a social network at their college in order to get dates, proving that you better be nice to nerds who dare to be ridiculous. Steve Jobs famously urged tech geeks of the world to "stay foolish."

You may be scratching your head and wondering what more you can do in addition to the mind-set shifts and strategies already covered, and you could be thinking, *Wow, I keep feeling blocked when I try taking action to give myself a needed boost.* If so, this might be the time to encourage you to let go of your fear of looking stupid.

Many of us are familiar with the fear of failure, or of being different, or not being accepted, or coming up with a dumb idea and being told, "No." I can suggest a few remedies.

* *Lighten up.* It's okay not to always take yourself too seriously. If you're worried someone is going to make fun of you, why not make a little fun of yourself? I used to be too mortified to tell people about my lack of education. Now I'm a hard-core self-educator, but I'm the first to say that I am the most brilliant uneducated person you'll ever meet.

* *Fail on purpose.* Free yourself from the pressure of having to be perfect all the time. Experiment with an idea in a safe space, maybe on your own time, and actually try to fail. When you get past the fear of all the terrible things

that can happen if you did look stupid, you can usually see that it's not the worst thing in the world.

* *Learn from past embarrassment and how you rebounded.* Think back to the most embarrassing thing you ever did. How bad was it really? You clearly survived, and maybe it's time to let that scar heal.

* *Adopt a "so what?" game face.* Have you ever decided just to not worry about what other people might think of you? Did you ever just go driving around your neighborhood with the windows down, blasting ridiculous old-school music? It's the best feeling in the world when you decide not to care. Once you practice not caring about something like being a little corny, you'll grow to like it—I promise.

In my experience, there is nothing that can stymie your creativity more than being afraid of looking dumb in the eyes of others. There are some fears we should heed, without a doubt. But when you want to act like an owner and launch a new venture of any kind, fear is not your friend. The two best ways to combat it are: (a) Let your hunger for something better help you see past your fear. And (b) Choose to be ridiculous in the face of your fear and see what happens.

I'm sure there were plenty of people at Frito-Lay who thought it was ridiculous for a janitor to run around taking notes in a notebook, and then writing up a report about cutting unnecessary waste. I'll bet they thought I was weird. The reactions I got all the time persuaded me to try out my bolder, crazier ideas in the privacy of my home office.

"What do you think?" I asked Judy when I first set up a drafting board and a desk in a corner of our small den.

She loved it. A home office made sense. There was nothing silly about looking for ways to add to the family income. Most of the people I knew in the hood could only make ends meet by having more than one job. So whether it was collecting, recharging, and selling used batteries, going door-to-door to take orders for Judy's homemade tortillas and salsa, jarring hot peppers, selling my horticultural services, or duplicating mixtapes of my eclectic music tastes, we tried it all.

When I say "we," I mean it literally. Judy, our two boys, and I (and later our third son) made it a family affair. Well, it was free labor, for one thing. More than that, as I became intent on developing and practicing my skills as an entrepreneur, I knew that building my own company required a team effort. My strategy was also to make sure we spent quality time together as a family.

We went all out. Whenever I came home from work, in the evening or much later if I was on a night shift, instead of kicking back, I'd change out of the clothes I'd worn to the plant and put on a business suit I'd bought at Goodwill. Next I'd grab a secondhand briefcase filled with important papers— notes, drawings, ideas for possible projects to pursue—and go straight to work in the corner of the home office. None of that may seem overly ridiculous to you, but I took it even further.

For instance, I had the audacity to come up with a company name for our family operation. We had not made any profit, but I was sure we would. Nothing gimmicky—going with our location and our main preoccupation, the research and development of a successful small business, I called us Rancho Cucamonga R & D. I printed up business cards, and using my artistic talents—inherited from my father—I designed a logo and silk-screened it onto T-shirts for Judy, the boys, and me. To anyone but us, I must have really looked *loco*.

Judy and I would go door-to-door with the boys (and later the baby too), all of us in our company T-shirts, selling or taking orders. Judy and the boys were a hit in their T-shirts, but I think I got a few laughs when I'd hand out a card—kind of ridiculous when the recipients already knew me by name.

Who cared? How else was I going to stand out? By this point, I'd convinced myself that a bigger, hotter revelation was on its way, and I wanted to be prepared to run with it. In this way, after practicing the art of seeing the unseen and creating opportunities for myself, I came to the conclusion that when my breakthrough idea came through, I'd recognize it because brilliance—like greatness—often comes in ridiculous forms.

Like most attempts to improve, the more you work at daring to be different, the better you get at it. It made me feel good to learn that ridiculousness is a certain sign of an entrepreneur. Even the word *entrepreneur* was itself slightly ridiculous. At the swap meet one day I mentioned that word to a friend to describe what I was—in addition to my work at Frito-Lay.

"Entre-pre . . . what?" my friend asked. I explained and he

asked how that was any different from being a hustler. He had a point. *Entrepreneur* was a fancy name for a hustler.

Etymologists trace it back to the middle of the eighteenth century when the king of Prussia wrote, "If the country happens not to abound in forage, you must agree with some Entrepreneur for the quantity required." During the nineteenth century, it was also described as "a go-between or a person who undertakes any kind of activity"* (as opposed to just a business). Eventually the word changed to refer to a go-getter when applied to an independent business owner, a quality that may also be found in the phrase *entrepreneurial spirit.*

We had some failures at Rancho Cucamonga R & D. Judy's salsa was a hit with everyone who tasted it, and her tortillas were in demand. But we overproduced and undersold. We'd donate what we didn't sell to help feed the hungry in the area, so it didn't go to waste completely—even when our cupboards were getting bare. There was no need to feel embarrassed about our failure—even though I knew people were making comments about how stupid it was to think we could really make money from that business.

Sometimes I did become discouraged. But then I'd go to the library, looking ridiculously overdressed in my Goodwill suit, and read up on famous entrepreneurs, and I'd learn that many of their ideas were absurd longshots. When Ray Kroc franchised and then bought a hamburger business from the

---

Online Etymology Dictionary, s.v. "entrepreneur (*n.*)," www.etymonline .com/word/entrepreneur.

McDonald brothers, he had visions of creating a national chain that at the time was a ridiculous pipedream. He was in his fifties, broke, in poor health, and hadn't done anything of note in his career. Within just a few years he had sold one hundred million hamburgers. The real genius of Ray Kroc and the team he built was to buy the land that McDonald's restaurants sat on. He built an empire based not only on food but on land.

I found example after example of different kinds of individuals who started something late in life and then became phenomenally successful. They gave me hope. Not that I was so old at twenty-eight, but I did sometimes feel stupid and like a failure for having left school at such a young age. That's one of my big messages to younger audiences, as it was to my sons and my grandchildren—*Stay in school, apply yourself and embrace every aspect of your education.* Maybe there's a little "Do as I *say*, not as I *do*" about this subject. Or in my case, not as I *did*.

The fact that today I can say I have done well without a formal education is yet another argument for going as far in school as you can. If I could accomplish a lot with only a sixth-grade education, think how much more successful you can be if you take advantage of every educational opportunity you get. During that time of trying to be a developer of offbeat, different ideas as a side hustle, I developed a greater appreciation for the years I spent learning in nontraditional "classrooms" that followed my leaving home at fourteen—working all kinds of jobs, going without creature comforts, riding the rails, foraging for food, listening to individuals who'd seen a side of life few of us ever see, and sleeping without a roof over your head, only a sky full of stars. I met more people and developed the ability to talk to just about anyone on their level while being free to be me.

The more I understood that greatness may come in ridiculous forms, the more I looked for evidence of it. I took comfort in the fact that the original founder of Fritos and the creator of Saratoga Chips had to get past their fear of looking stupid. C. E. Doolin wanted a salty corn snack for a store that sold sweets. How dumb is that? The chef who created potato chips did so just to annoy Cornelius Vanderbilt and became a legend in the process.

The saga that fascinated me more than anything was that of Roger Enrico, the very CEO of Pepsi who would later send out his video asking for every employee to act like an owner. His story was full of moments when he threw off his fears of looking ridiculous and dared to take decisive action that paid off time and again.

At twenty-six, a college graduate and navy veteran who'd served in Vietnam and hadn't gone the usual route to an Ivy League MBA, Roger Enrico left a brand management job at General Mills to work for Frito-Lay. Within eleven years, his bold leadership style had put him at the helm of PepsiCo. This was when the epic Cola Wars were escalating. Pepsi was in trouble, about to lose disastrously.

Everything Enrico did to orchestrate a win for Pepsi versus Coke was strategic yet seen as outrageous and even ridiculous—from taking over every detail of the Pepsi Generation ad campaign to signing Michael Jackson (then the biggest pop star in the world) to one of the most highly priced endorsement deals in any brand's history. When Roger heard an idea for a taste test to be billed as a battle of the colas, he pounced on it and promoted the Pepsi Challenge as the underdog story of going up against Coke, the heavyweight cola champion of the world. Skeptics worried that if you challenged consumers to do a blind taste test to compare Pepsi with Coke, the results could hurt. Roger believed that wasn't a problem because just getting in the ring with number one would put Pepsi in a whole new class.

Coca-Cola freaked out and developed the disastrous New Coke. They were so afraid of losing and looking ridiculous that they didn't bother to ask their loyal customers if they were unhappy with the taste of Coke. New Coke was soon considered one of the costliest blunders of product marketing. Soon there was a rift between New Coke and Classic Coke. Some Coca-Cola fans felt betrayed. Roger upped the ante by sending out press releases calling New Coke dead on arrival. He played it like a heavyweight champ would before getting into the ring and declared Pepsi the winner before the taste challenge was concluded, saying, "After 87 years of going at it eyeball to eyeball, the other guy just blinked."

When the Pepsi Challenge was done, with Classic Coke declared the number one best-tasting cola, it was all still worth it. Pepsi sales jumped dramatically as the number two beloved cola the world over. Roger Enrico then began an ambitious global program to expand PepsiCo's family of brands (with beverage, food, snack, and restaurant divisions), making it the unrivaled winning superbrand. None of the brands were as profitable as Frito-Lay, the crown jewel.

It was at a moment after it had become clear that the crunchy snack division was ailing that Roger came up with his video appeal to all of us. Was it ridiculous for me to think he was telling me, the janitor, that I was as likely as anyone else to come up with an idea that could help the corporation? Probably. Would throwing my hat in the ring as an inventor make me look ridiculous? Definitely.

Was I afraid to try? Absolutely not. I'd been doing my homework and had been in training to get past my fear of looking dumb. So can you. It's not easy, I know, but let me offer some suggestions to help you engage your natural gift of ridiculousness.

In almost every instance when I decided to be an entrepreneur willing to not care what others thought, I did so by first letting myself dream. Some of us can remember what it was like to daydream as a kid. Yet some of us, like me, had to grow up too fast in order to survive, and we didn't learn how to be silly and fanciful. However, as I learned in my twenties when I had kids of my own, it's never too late to practice dreaming of possibilities as ridiculously as you please. Give some of these exercises a try:

* *Dream on.* Wherever you are in your life, think back to a time when you used to daydream about who you wanted to be one day or what you wanted to do. Maybe it was years ago or last month. When I left home in my teens to support

myself, I used daydreams to imagine a better future. Food and rent were my dreams. Later, when I went to work, I didn't always love my job, so I daydreamed of being a leader who would offer wise counsel to my community. I daydreamed of having classic cars and souped-up motorcycles and a big house and land where I could grow all kinds of exotic trees and plants. Was that foolish? Maybe. But if it was only in my head, nobody had to know. Because I could see all of these things in my mind, I began to believe the fantasy could be real. So daydream, fantasize, and cook up a great story for yourself.

* *Dress-up is for grown-ups too.* As a kid I used to love to put on costumes and play at being superheroes or firefighters or cultural figures. Many adults I know love Halloween and other opportunities to dress up for special occasions. There is something that happens inside of you when you give yourself permission to act and dress in ways that let you feel cool and attractive, even though they may seem silly or inappropriate to others. How ridiculous for a factory worker to wear a suit and tie to work at home, right? Dress for your dreams.

* *Rewrite your own story.* I love reading stories about famous entrepreneurs who had never been very successful and then decided they would rewrite their history so that the next chapter would be their own happily ever after. How ridiculous that someone without a track record would decide their next chapter was going to have it all—fame, fortune, love, accomplishment, social impact, and so on. If you haven't been letting yourself daydream of how to

win in the next installment of your story, challenge yourself to do it right now. You hold the pen.

Where would any of us be in this world without dreamers?
Where would entrepreneurs, inventors, and innovators be
without dreams? Let yourself dream as ridiculously as you
want about how it would feel to win at something huge. So
what if you feel uncomfortable pushing yourself to dream?
If a dream isn't crazy and it doesn't scare you, then it's not
really a dream.

The bottom line is that when you declare that you are ready
for your own revelation that can lead to a revolution, you've
already got the stuff to sideline your fears. Like most innovators and entrepreneurs who make it big, you're at an advantage if you've faced a series of failures, disappointments, and
obstacles. You've most likely had moments when you looked
foolish to others, and you've learned to take it in stride or to
get up off the ground, dust off, and move on.

My money is on you to win. Now it's time to use a strategy
that combines most of what we've talked about so far.

6

The Power of "What If? What Then?" Makes It Worth the Risk

For most of my life I've lived a little more than an hour outside of Hollywood.

Even so, it was always as distant to me as Jupiter or Mars. Not that I was a country bumpkin. In fact, I am one of the hungriest consumers of Hollywood's products—movies, TV, and, especially, music. And you know what? I may be from the barrio, but I've got good taste. Always have.

Still, everything in that world—show business—was a distant galaxy from mine. The mansions, the fancy cars, the movie stars—none of that seemed real. Here I was, this kid who grew up in a migrant farm camp, dropped out of school by the sixth grade to go work with adults three times my age, got in fights, got in trouble, rode the rails, and slept out under the stars talking philosophy with crazy characters like a Latino Tom Sawyer. That same kid had wound up settling down with a good woman, had kids, got a job as a janitor but started to act like an owner and had a revelation based on a wild premise that had turned into a global snack revolution—namely, "What if I put chili on a Cheeto?"

Obviously, I would never have anything in common with Hollywood, right?

Then again, you never know. Truth really is often stranger than fiction. And it turns out that Hollywood loves to tell unbelievable but true stories. So just as we've been discussing, there's nothing wrong with asking a ridiculous question: *What if my story could be a movie one day?*

From what I've learned lately, it also turns out that in coming up with new, exciting premises, the big honchos in Hollywood often employ those simple two words put together—*what* and *if*. We've talked about the viability of ideas, no matter how small, that solve problems, fill a need, or are just ridiculous enough to get the attention of others. There are two aspects of idea creation and promotion that we have yet to fully explore: (1) putting a personal spin on your "what if" ideas and how you plan to show them to decision makers, and (2) applying the question "what then" to overcome hurdles on your way to turning your ideas into something real.

When you give your "what if" your own stamp and decide you like it as a premise, you'll get the wheels turning when you ask yourself, "What then?" It's a reality check that gets you thinking about what you or your company or investors have to do to bring it to life. That involves a commodity known as *risk*. This can be the do-or-die element in your success.

Now that I've had a chance to learn a little about the development process in the entertainment industry, I can say with full authority that the risk-taking strategies are the same in multimillion-dollar major endeavors as they are with the small improvements you implement on the job or build in your garage. None of these undertakings are very different from research and development in the food and beverage industry. All industries use some form of "what if and what then"—from show business to shoe business, whatever the arena, whenever and wherever there is a desire for innovation and creativity, and for turning something that exists in theory into reality.

Let's look more closely at the question of how you decide which big ideas are worth the risk of your time, money, and reputation.

Stephen King's response on his website to the frequently asked question of where he gets his ideas is this:

> What all of my ideas boil down to is seeing maybe one thing, but in a lot of cases it's seeing two things and having them come together in some new and interesting way, and then adding the question "What if?" "What if" is always the key question.*

It's like a chemical compound. When two unrelated things come together in an exciting collision, it makes for something that warrants a risk. How do you know? Usually you have a gut-check moment. Almost every great business success story

*Stephen King, "Frequently Asked Questions," accessed March 24, 2001, https://stephenking.com/faq.

I've ever heard includes a moment when one person saw the unseen by bringing together two things already seen and then asking, "What if?"—a creative catalyst to their big revelation. Albert Einstein asked, "*What if* I could ride a beam of light?" His "what then" was to work out the astrophysics and mechanics of that preposterous question to invent his most famous equation, $E = mc^2$.

The theory of special relativity, as it is known, connected two things—space and time, as both apply to objects moving in a direct line. He also threw gravity in the mix. The equation says that *energy* (E) is equal to the *mass* (m) times the *speed of light squared* (c^2). In the world of science and our understanding of atomic energy, it doesn't get any more revolutionary than that. The *risk* component of acting on his developed premise involved science and a gut check. Einstein had to know he was about to upend the scientific world.

The beauty of "what if" is that it is a self-empowering spark for creativity. It lets you think outside the box, as we used to say. Or without any box at all. It lets you throw in your own style and sensibilities—what you can even call your own "brand." When you feel free enough to come up with a few ideas, often one of them will jump out as the hot idea that has your name on it. Or maybe your "what if" is too all over the place. Can you rein it in and make it more practical? In brainstorming sessions in which I've participated and those I've facilitated, there are two other small words that can also come into play when you wonder just how viable the idea is and how risky it can be. The words are *why* and *not*.

Whenever you get bogged down in thinking about the risk

of moving forward with an idea, asking yourself "Why not?" is the equivalent of giving yourself a pep talk and responding, "What's the worst that could happen?" or "What do I have to lose?" You've empowered yourself to take a leap into the unknown with your question "What *then*?"

The secret I eventually learned that would have helped me even before I came up with my big "what if"—What if I put chili on a Cheeto?—is that the so-called powers that be who can say yay or nay to your idea are actually in the position of asking "What if?" and "What then?" to solve their own needs every day. The higher you get on the totem pole, the bigger the risk because you have to make decisions that affect your entire workforce and your shareholders. You have to sometimes roll the dice. If you're smart about it, you'll reap the rewards.

No one I've ever observed was better at being smart about rolling the dice than Roger Enrico. It took me years to appreciate that when he decided to make a video asking everyone in the company to act like an owner, he was risking his stature as one of the most admired business CEOs in America. He was problem solving and going against the grain by posing the question "What if the solution to our slumping sales could come from any one of our employees?"

Roger Enrico must have been as concerned as we were about the hours being cut from production and the resulting toll on families like mine. Besides the slump in production, at this point in the latter half of the 1980s the "trickle down" from a strong economy for some had not made it into the pockets of lower-level hourly workers—like janitors.

If we were feeling desperate, I had to imagine that the person tasked with recharging Frito-Lay must have been too. My hunch is after Roger put the question to himself—*What if we asked everyone in the company (all three hundred thousand employees) to step up*—his next question was "What then?" The answer was to send out a message company-wide in the form of a video that gave everyone the power to make a difference.

That was life changing for me. But the truth is I was already toying with ideas I hoped could become revelations. The point to remember is that you may not always have a CEO or boss who will empower you to be creative and take risks, but you can always use the questions that powerful leaders use—*What if? Why not? What then?*

Can you imagine the Hollywood pitch? *What if* a janitor and a visionary top executive of one of the world's largest food and beverage corporations teamed up to empower every working person everywhere to think and act like an owner?

Well, *why not*? What then?

THE TIMING WAS GOOD. BY NOW I HAD BEEN IN THE HABIT OF LOOKING for opportunities to create for myself while acting like an owner, thinking like an executive, and practicing the art of not being afraid to be ridiculous. The thing that was still missing, though, was the *Big One*, the impactful revelation that could lead to more work at the plant for all of us. Soon. It was out there just hovering around me, nearby, and if I closed my eyes, it was something I could almost touch and taste. Whenever I prayed about it, a calm would come over me, a kind of reassurance that told me the planets would align any day and all would be well.

Then one night, not too long before my twenty-ninth birthday, Judy and I watched an old movie with Jimmy Stewart on TV. Released in February 1954, it was *The Glenn Miller Story*, and was more or less true—from his early struggles trying to find success as a musician to how he turned it all around with one of the most popular big bands of his time.

The movie fit into my project, as an entrepreneur, of collecting stories of success. Some of them came from classic books like Og Mandino's *The Greatest Salesman in the World* and later from *The Alchemist* by Paulo Coelho. I also learned about overcoming the odds from heroes in the movies. At first, Jimmy Stewart, as Glenn Miller, couldn't seem to catch a break, no matter how talented he was. He wrote and arranged songs beautifully, had great musicians in his band, and sounded like all the most popular big bands. But that was the problem. He didn't have his own sound—his signature.

You know how when you hear Aretha Franklin sing two notes, they can't be from anyone but her? When you hear a guitar riff from Carlos Santana, it can only be his sound, nobody else's. In the movie, Glenn Miller couldn't figure out what to do to get his own sound. Then one night when he had a show scheduled, his trumpet player hurt his lip and couldn't play. Glenn was stuck. He had to act like the owner because he was the leader of the band. The other musicians were depending on him. Out of desperation, he picked up one of the instruments he played well but that wasn't usually part of the mix and asked, "What if I played the trombone?"

That was it. Magic. He found his sound and, of course, everything he had worked so hard to make happen finally fell into place. For three years he was one of the most successful recording artists around.

After watching the movie, I could barely sleep that night. In the morning, I told Judy that everything I needed for success was already within my means—the only thing missing was my sound. I believed wholeheartedly that I was not meant to fit in but rather to stand out. I believed that instead of standing in the line others had put me in, I'd need to break ranks and go to the line I wanted to be in. But still, what was it that made my ideas different and authentic?

Judy's advice was not to keep looking in all the same places. "Isn't that what you always tell me?"

True, I usually would say that if you choose to change your perspective, you'll see things differently.

For the next few days, as I thought about my new insight from Glenn Miller, I started to reflect on aspects of food, family, and culture that made me feel at home and gave me joy. My gut check told me that somehow, my sound and signature for the *Big One* would have to do with who I am.

That was my thinking the very next morning when Julius

called me to watch the video from HQ, and a few days later when I took myself out of my usual setting on our sales route. My flamin' hot idea began with a "what if" I did something with spices from my culture. . . . putting them on a chip? Of course! That would be my sound, my signature! If it were my company, why would I offer any other flavors but the ones I'd grown up savoring? Then I refined it a week later when I saw José selling corn on a stick with all the trimmings and it looked like a Cheeto. And that's how I put my spin on a great premise—"*What if* I put chili on a Cheeto?"

Why not? What then? Empowered, my home team—my wife, Judy, my sons Lucky, Steven, and baby Mike—then went to work, and soon Rancho Cucamonga R & D had cooked up a prototype to demonstrate the idea for decision makers.

Now that I had found my sound, my signature for bringing the spices of my background to others who shared my culture as well as to others who didn't, I felt empowered enough to risk making the call to Roger Enrico.

THE ROLE OF LEADERS IN EMPOWERING THOSE WHO FOLLOW THEM IS not as controversial as it once was. In the old command and control structure that most companies followed, it was considered risky to empower lower-level employees. The hierarchy was like the military. Officers gave the orders while the lower ranks followed them. No wiggle room.

Command and control is never good for creativity and imagination. There are reasons for that. Around running machinery, workers who want to get creative can pose all kinds of hazards if they don't follow the rules. However, it never made any sense to me when I was working on money-saving projects for the company that managers would bark, "We're not paying you to learn to use the computer. Do what we pay you to do."

Roger Enrico had decided to upend the command and control system to empower everyone to think and act independently. That was a risk. Take a look at the meaning and etymology of the word *empower*:

> **Definition:** To give someone more control over their life or more power to do something.
>
> **Origin and usage:** The word *empower* comes from the Old French prefix *en-* meaning "in, into" and the root *power*, which comes from the early 1300s, meaning "ability, strength, might." Though the word *empower* has been used in the past in literary works, its modern usage dates from around 1986.*

As you can see, it wasn't until 1986—in the same era when the first Flamin' Hot Cheeto came out of our kitchen lab—that the word *empower* began to be used as we think of it now. Roger Enrico deserves a lot of credit for that.

Macmillan Dictionary Blog, "Word of the Day: empower," www.macmillan dictionaryblog.com/empower.

The more time has gone on, the more grateful I am for the challenges and pushback I've experienced with my earlier, smaller "what if" projects. In the past I'd been naive to think that everyone would cheer on good ideas that were going to help all of us. This time, I knew better. But I still find it shocking how close I came to being stopped from making the do-or-die phone call to Frito-Lay headquarters.

With two exceptions, I didn't tell any of the managers. Management knew me and had warned me before that as an hourly worker, I was not to do any extra work when I was on the clock. The concept of my acting like an owner, obviously, was a threat to their sense of the command and control hierarchy. The thing that posed an even bigger threat was that I knew more about the entire operation of our plant than they did.

My instincts told me that how the managers reacted wasn't my problem. Maybe that was a risk because I'd gone over their heads before and there'd been repercussions. Though I was naive in other ways, including the fact that I had no clue you weren't supposed to pick up the phone and call headquarters, I wasn't going to tell the managers about hot Cheetos.

Later, when I was forced to tell them, the managers were predictably appalled. They lost their minds. "What do you think you're doing? That is so sacrilegious, you want to put chili on the Cheeto? Why would you ever do that? You're going to ruin the brand. Are you serious?"

They weren't visionary. Most visionaries are five to ten years ahead of everyone. They couldn't see the potential. Out of reflex, I wanted to just get into an old-fashioned fight, but that was no longer who I was. I had to remember that I wasn't the one with the problem. From then on, I resolved to live by the belief that you must never lower yourself to make somebody feel good about themselves.

There were two managers I chose to confide in. Julius knew what was up from the start. He was a visionary and predicted that even if it took a while to win approval, this spicy Cheeto was going to help save Frito-Lay. There was another manager who took me into his confidence, warning me that I would upset the status quo but that my creation was exactly what the company needed. Part of the leadership team who groomed future executives, he didn't call himself my mentor, but he had my back. He was the first person to warn me that I was seen as a threat and some managers would look for any opportunity to get me fired. We used to talk in secret. He offered the most tactical guidance I'd been given. If I was working on something, he'd say, "Let's go outside," and he would lay things out for me.

In the middle of those two weeks in which Flamin' Hot Cheetos were conceived, developed, and born, before anyone knew anything, this particular manager had pulled me outside and said, "Richard, you're making everybody nervous, and they're watching you, so be careful. They're looking for opportunities to get you. They're watching your time clock. Make sure you don't overextend your lunch. Make sure you're not late. Make sure you leave when you're supposed to."

I thanked him for risking his own security by telling me.

God must have been watching out for me by sending

that message. This guy knew that I was empowered, but, as a messenger, he had to make sure I watched my own back. As I've commented before, there is someone always in the room ready to steal your destiny, and I don't care what room it is. Letting my guard down, I assumed we were all working for the same cause.

All of this made the decision to call Roger Enrico more of a risk.

After discussing it late into the night with Judy, I woke up early the next morning after not too much sleep and suddenly remembered Al Carey, who had given me his card and said I could call him anytime. In a *"what if, why not, what then"* moment, I picked up the phone at home and dialed the number on the card.

"Richard, great to hear from you," Al said right away, with that same warmth I recalled from the time we had met in person.

I told him what I had going and then announced, "I'm calling them Flamin' Hot Cheetos."

"Sounds great!" Al said, excited. "How can I help?" When I reminded him of the video, he said that, yes, they were looking for ideas like mine.

"Do you think I should call Mr. Enrico directly?"

Al Carey paused and then said, "Why not? Why don't you tell Roger about your product. You can tell him that I said you should call. Mention my name."

If I had ever doubted the fact that it's not who you know but who knows you, here was proof positive. When I put down the receiver, I was even more empowered. All I had to do was be myself. If the CEO wasn't interested, it would be their loss, and I'd try another approach.

After my shift was over, I stopped in at what was then the business, accounting, and secretarial office. This was in the days before cubicles, so all of the clerical staff were in a pool, working away at various desks. As I walked in, the head office manager asked, "Something you need?"

"I was just looking for the company directory."

Everyone seemed to stop their work to glare at me. Were they that annoyed about a directory? We didn't have email, so if you needed to contact anyone in the company, there was an interoffice phone system.

The head of the clerical team handed me the directory but with a huffy tone was quick to tell me, "This is only for company use, you know."

Politely I said that this *was* company business, that I needed to call the CEO.

"Oh," she said, eyebrows raised, "you can go ahead and use my phone." She smiled and everyone lowered their faces, kind of looking at the person next to them, and then went back to work, apparently no longer interested.

Only later did I realize that the clerical manager wanted me to use her phone because calling the CEO and breaking protocol was something that could get me fired for causing trouble. Instead of saying, *Who do you think you are, coming in here and putting me in an embarrassing position when this comes back to get me chewed out?* she went in the other direction and decided to be an eyewitness to it all. If I had paid better attention, I would have picked up on the whispers of *Oh, his ass is going to get fired!* They had apparently never seen anybody canned on the spot before and must have been as excited as the crowds in the Roman Colosseum.

Only vice presidents called the CEO and only for an emergency. Command and control hierarchy was a lot like the military. A private had no rights to approach a general without speaking to an immediate supervisor. Clearly, I was breaking rank, defying the status quo—even if the word *protocol* wasn't in my vocabulary at the time.

Already nervous as I made the call, I again give enormous credit to the CEO's executive assistant, Patti—and I have to stress the word *executive* because she was the gatekeeper who could have easily turned me away. But she must have heard something in my voice and was willing to risk her job, her stature, and her boss's estimation of her judgment by getting Roger Enrico on the phone.

There were some surprised reactions in the room around me when they heard me thank Patti for getting Mr. Enrico and say that I'd be happy to hold. All I could do was be myself. For some reason, I thought back to my Guasti days at the dinner table and how I did have a gift for gab. My gut told me to just get to my point and see what he thought.

The critical moment arrived when Mr. Enrico picked up the phone, wasted no time in asking what he could do for me, and paid close attention as I reminded him about the video—and how it inspired me to come up with an idea for a product I'd developed.

Roger Enrico listened with some interest, respectfully, of course, but it wasn't until I said, "You know, a while back I saw Al Carey at the plant—"

"Oh, you know Al Carey?" Now the CEO became animated.

Joking a little, I said, "Well, Al Carey knows me."

Roger laughed with gusto.

"Anyway," I went on, "I told him about this new product and he said to call you."

The rest of the conversation became a happy blur until he announced that he would fly out to the plant in a couple weeks and would like to see a presentation.

A presentation? In my mind, this would involve tapping a couple of the experienced managers at the plant who would come around to seeing my innovation as a good thing for all of us. Little did I know that all hell was about to break loose as word got out that a janitor had broken protocol and called the CEO.

WHEREVER YOU ARE IN YOUR JOURNEY TO ATTAIN YOUR HIGHEST aspirations or just the immediate goals you care about now, I believe that your ability to take smart risks can determine how far you can go and how fast you can get there.

How do you get past your own reluctance to take the risks? How do you tell a smart risk from a risky risk? How do you test your ideas and decisions before you look at the risk? Let's look again at the tools at your disposal:

1. *Start from an empowered place.* Did you ever go out and march for a cause or work for something that you cared about more than anything? If so, can you remember how powerful that made you feel? When you are empowered, by a boss, a teacher, a loved one who believes in you, by your spiritual adviser or your higher power, that conviction can be valuable for overcoming your reluctance to take a risk. When you go out of your way to stand up for something you believe in, that's taking power away from the powers that be. You get a feeling that tells you that even if your risk fails, it doesn't matter because you gave it your all and tasted the feeling of being empowered.

Whenever I thought about becoming a success, I would think back to my youth in the late '60s and early '70s, a time of civil rights marches, protests against the Vietnam War, and important voices that included three of my heroes: Cesar Chavez, Dr. Martin Luther King Jr., and Muhammad Ali. My awareness of injustice had begun as I watched how migrant farmworkers were disrespected by people higher up on the socioeconomic ladder. Why was it tolerable to disregard and demean people—African Americans, Hispanics, Native Americans, Asians, and others—who were trying to attain a small piece of the American dream? What birthright gave those high and mighty people the privilege to enjoy the fruits of our labors but then show no respect to workers who toiled at the kind of menial jobs I worked in those years—pulling weeds, picking grapes, planting trees, washing cars, killing chickens? My indignation empowered me, and if I had the chance to do something to achieve my aspirations, in ways to help others too, then the risk was nothing to me.

2. *Trust your instincts.* We are all born with an inner guidance system that warns us of danger and leads us to food, shelter, love, and opportunity. It's your inner GPS that can help you decide whether your risk is a smart one or one that will not serve you over the long haul. If you want to change your career, leave a job, choose a side hustle that could become your main hustle, check your GPS for which one is the smartest risk. Sometimes your instincts will tell you to hold tight and revisit the question later.

3. *Do your own research and development on your idea and direction.* The secret formula for R & D is to start your idea or plan with testing. Research other options with "what if" and "why not" questions. If you can refine the idea, that will make it an even smarter risk. Make sure there is a demand in the marketplace and that you aren't duplicating someone else's successful idea. Or make sure you have a "signature sound" that will let your concept shine. Now test it out even further with a "what then" question. What is going to be involved to bring this idea to life? Who is going to do it and how much will it cost?

Empowerment is like a shield of armor that can counter all those naysayers who want you to fail. The risk is always going to be real, but if all systems are go, you are ready for a flamin' hot adventure. What else do you want?

That's how I felt when I got off the phone with Roger Enrico—that an adventure was in store. My instincts told me that big things were happening and that my real work was about to begin.

7

Creating Your Flamin' Hot Sales Pitch

There comes a moment in every mountain climber's journey when you finally get to a place halfway up and it's way more steep than you ever imagined. All this time you were moving up, stretching from one rock to another, not really thinking about what it was going to take to make it all the way to the top. You arrive at a small landing, so excited about your progress, and then you look up to see a straight sheet of rock that you have no idea how to scale. Nobody ever told you about this stage of climbing. You look down and there's no turning back because you'd set off a rock slide below you. What *now*?

For a lot of us—whether you're determined to go from your revelation toward your revolution as an entrepreneur, or looking for investors for your company or your product, or trying to get a better job or promotion—this is the big test.

Many people don't realize that there is a significant learning curve when it comes to having to go out and pitch yourself or your idea to others and prove that it and/or you are an opportunity for them too. Once you have the potential for interest or that proverbial door has been opened, you will need a plan, proposal, or presentation you can use to communicate how you're going to scale the much tougher terrain coming up.

If you find yourself in this position, don't feel alone. You are not! A lot of us start our climbs and push forward against the odds only to get to a place where more planning and work are required. You know, the hard part of being a visionary is tuning out all those negative voices telling you that you're ridiculous and asking, *Who do you think you are?* Or in my case, *We don't pay you to create new products! Make sure you clock out!*

When you're making your big pitch, you just need to find a way to communicate how you can add value to the goals of your manager, company, or customer. It's actually quite simple:

1. Focus on the *Need* or *Demand* for whatever you're offering as a *Solution*.
2. Innovation is important, but don't be too radical; combine *Familiarity* with your *Novelty*.

Bind these two principles together with a great story, and you're set. The only reason I survived the uproar at Frito-Lay after I called Roger Enrico with my Flamin' Hot Cheetos idea was because of this strategy.

AFTER PATTI, ROGER ENRICO'S EXECUTIVE ASSISTANT, DID ME THE unforgettable favor of putting my call through and then he said, "I'll be there in two weeks," I felt detached from the ground—as if I were on a cloud! Let me repeat, I had no idea what *protocol* even meant or that I was about to cause a corporation-wide hissy fit.

Meanwhile, the head of the business office and the clerical staff were sending me curious glances. They were being all-out nosy but in a subtle way—so that I wasn't supposed to see that they weren't minding their own business. They had only heard my side of the conversation, and seemed to have been whispering the whole time. But before anyone could ask me a thing, I returned the company directory and walked out.

Before long, the plant manager came screaming in my direction. In those days you could scream at employees and get away with it.

"Montañez, who the hell do you think you are?"

My first reaction was confusion. If my ideas went up the chain, didn't they make everyone else look good? My assumption would have been right if we truly were a team. But that was not at all the case, made plain by the volume of the plant manager's voice.

Later it would become clear that Roger Enrico himself must have called the Frito-Lay president, who in turn called the senior vice president, who called the California president, and all the way down the line. The conversation must have been the same, starting with the question, "Who let the janitor call the CEO? Who is this Richard Montañez?"

No doubt there were a lot of executives on the plant manager's ass. As a result, he had it in for me in a way he never had before. "Now I have to paint the place!" he said, looking at me in disgust. "We have to clean it all up and give a tour!" He started to walk away and then added, "And you're going to give the presentation yourself." He spun on his heel, grinning.

My first reaction was shock. It had never occurred to me that I would have to make an official presentation for an innovation that was developed to help my company. My next reaction, however, was to get mad and take this as a challenge.

The plant manager's tone told me everything—that he believed I would fall on my face, and my ridiculous endeavor would for sure be a failure. There was no way in his view that an uneducated Chicano son of migrant farmworkers like me, who'd never given a company-wide presentation, could pull this thing off. He relished the thought of my making a fool of myself in front of the CEO—who in turn would blame me for dragging him all the way to California.

I rushed home to talk to Judy, who saw the horrified look on my face.

"What's wrong?"

"I'm gonna get fired," I announced.

"Why?"

"Because I called the CEO." Judy's confused reaction prompted me to say, "I did what you told me to do and now I'm in trouble."

Judy stayed cool and swung right into action. We went immediately to the library and checked out three books on marketing strategies. One in particular was a book about sales pitches and in it were three paragraphs as an example that I could pretty much borrow and use to show that I had a plan for how this product would *add value* to the entire Frito-Lay and Pepsi family of product lines. When you want someone to say yes to you or your project or your business idea, your most important task is to show how it's going to add value to enterprises that already exist for that person (or that company).

First, I had to tell a story about how the need for Flamin' Hot was big and important. Flamin' Hot Cheetos weren't there to fix something that was broken, of course, or to replace classic Cheetos. My concept was for us to reach new consumers who wanted an alternative, consumers we were missing out on. My goal was to make everyone in that room, even the ones who found innovation threatening, to understand how much money there was to be made here.

I wanted to use both verbal and visual drama to have people on the edge of their seats. They needed to feel that if Frito-Lay didn't move quickly, we'd be missing out on responding to this void in the marketplace.

I already knew what the room I'd be presenting in—the

lion's den—looked like, having been inside it on prior occasions. It sat about one hundred people and had audio-visual capabilities complete with a lectern, a mic, an overhead projector, and a screen.

To have my product presented as if it were already on its way to the marketplace, I didn't want to hand out samples in plain old plastic snack bags. Not in this beautiful room. Going for excitement, I designed a logo: a fun little red baby devil on a black background with flames coming off him and his pitchfork. In those days, the mascot for Chee-tos (the way they used to spell the name) was a mouse who was into cheese. They hadn't yet phased in Chester Cheetah. With my home team assembly line helping, I drew the logo with multimedia markers on drawing paper, then cut the "label" out and glued each piece onto one hundred plastic bags. Man, I'd come a long way from the time when my teacher told me I couldn't draw because of my broken crayons!

Once we had filled the bags with Cheetos from a fresh batch of *Flamin' Hots* (as I first pitched them), we set out an assembly line on our ironing board and I sealed each bag shut with a warm iron, so there was nothing that looked makeshift about it. Being an entrepreneur, I dug into the little I had in my own pocket—probably skipping a couple of bills for that week—and went to a local print shop, where we mocked up a series of transparencies.

The story I'd decided to tell was about a party everybody was invited to attend—a celebration of Latino food and culture. The company was currently missing out on that party. Who wants to miss a party? The picture I drew on the transparency—a sheet of plastic that is placed on the glass base of an overhead projector that shows an image on the screen—was of a banner in the colors of the Mexican flag that read "Ven a La Fiesta," translated below on a gold banner: "Come to the Party!" Underneath the banners I drew a cheerful host with a sombrero and a tray of Flamin' Hots welcoming everyone to the experience that was going to be delicious and fun.

Covering all my bases, and then some, I assembled about fifteen three-ring binders that each held the same content as the PowerPoint to be shown on the transparencies, in case the real decision makers were back in Dallas and needed notes brought back to them.

In making sure my presentation would hit the right notes, I consulted my mentor Julius, who emphasized something I'd later hear much more about from top marketing experts— what some call the USP of a product, company, or service you are presenting. Julius was always ahead of the game. This concept applies to any scale of innovation or solution you may be pitching to a supervisor or executive where you work or to anyone you hope to sign on to a project.

The USP is the unique selling point (or points) that can be used to overcome most objections. Decision makers want to know what makes the thing that's being pitched really different. What is it that makes it "heroic" in terms of how consumers respond to it? Carmakers always give names to automobiles that are heroic and that conjure feelings of power and performance on the road. *Impala. Mustang. Cutlass. Cougar.* The USP should suggest those qualities and may even lead to a tagline. In pitching, the USP can make all the difference. You can think about it by asking yourself, *What is it that makes my product so unique that it will get headlines and create a buzz? When you hear the name and feel as if you're going to be invited to a party, that gives you a personal relationship to the product.* After all, in a crowded marketplace, everyone will want to know how you will grab that huge level of attention that's so important for launching something new. When corporate executives or independent investors watch countless presentations or read loads of business plans, the USPs are the things they'll remember that make your effort stand out. Again, you don't want to be so familiar that you blend in with everybody else's approach. You don't want to be so extreme that it appears risky.

With Flamin' Hot Cheetos, my belief was that I had three strong USPs. I didn't have to be a marketing expert to know that most major brands were just starting to realize the buying power of Latino consumers. Who better to come up with a product to appeal to those consumers than someone who was authentically one of them? I tracked down some data and turned it into a graph showing the estimated number of Latinos in the United States (twenty-two million in the late 1980s) and the projected increase for the next decade of almost 58 percent (up to nearly thirty-five million by the late 1990s). The idea of a culture known for its heat and sizzle was embedded in my product name and had that heroic quality that made you feel—*Wow, if I eat this Cheeto, I'm going to be flamin' hot!*

In the second place, if our executives missed the opportunity to run with a product that was already developed—on my time and on my dime—they would be throwing away millions of dollars they would otherwise need to spend on the R & D of any other new project. My family team and I had already accomplished everything that normally would take five to ten years of research and development, with PhD food scientists and numbers crunchers and marketing executives micromanaging every aspect of it, not to mention millions of dollars for outside branding and advertising gurus to prepare for a rollout. Flamin' Hot Cheetos could be rolled out and tested in stores and niche markets within three or four months.

Third, I knew that a common strategy for developing new products in-house was to send food scientists into restaurants to study popular dishes and figure out how to turn them into snacks. That's how a product like Doritos nacho chips had come to be. There was nothing authentically "nacho" about them, for sure, because they were just chips with a seasoning that had little to do with Mexican flavoring. Flamin' Hot Cheetos offered the same "meal in a snack" as a selling point and captured the real heat of our cuisine.

My pitch also proposed four different "strengths" of Cheetos with spice—Mild, Regular, Hot, and Extra Hot. The *Hot* version was what I'd spent time developing and what we'd packed and sealed in the bags for the attendees at the presentation to sample. So far, the reaction to the heat from friends and coworkers, predominantly Latino and African American, had been mostly a chorus of "just right," but I wasn't so sure about the palates of those not used to varying grades of spice. That's why, to be on the safe side, I proposed a future plan to go even hotter, plus versions slightly less hot all the way down to mild.

As the big day got closer, I felt my fear rising incrementally. Then I'd remind myself of all the lessons learned, allowing my hunger to be the antidote to the fear and putting on my best "So what? Who cares?" game face. That helped for the most part, but before long I'd start to shake just thinking about standing up in front of corporate heavyweights and having it be a total disaster. One afternoon, with only two days to go, I had a visit from the leadership adviser, who wasn't supposed to be helping me. He stopped by the custodial office and nodded to the door. We went outside and he reconfirmed—"They're definitely watching you, looking for any reason to fire you. They're still investigating your time card."

"My time card?" It made no sense. I'd been punching out and doing all the preparation work on my own time. You'd think they'd cut me a little slack for trying to do something to create more hours for frontline workers and for them. All my friend could do was tell me to make sure I knocked my presentation out of the park. The word was that there were a lot of managers looking forward to watching me blow it badly in front of the CEO.

"What should I do?" I asked.

"Don't blow it."

That was when I came up with a revelation for how to take over the room. It began with a memory from my adventuresome days as a teenager who slept under the stars and sat with amazing storytellers who would hold everyone spellbound. One of the best storytellers I ever heard was a white guy, a wino, who told some tall tales, but you believed every word and didn't care because he was so engaging. He watched you the whole time, gauging your reaction, and spoon-fed you his story, making sure he kept you engaged. He told stories about his time in the air force back in the Korean War, and about the importance of being authentic because you didn't owe the world an explanation. The gist of the word *authentic* was clear, though I later looked up the etymology and saw that among its sources was the Greek *authentes*, "one acting on one's own authority," and later a sense of "real, entitled to acceptance as factual."*

That sense of being authentic was something I wanted to bring to my sales pitch, just being myself, being real, but also demonstrating that I knew my stuff because it was gained from my experience. The one thing the storytelling character used to do was at a certain point in the story he'd pull out a prop that proved a point or that convinced you everything had happened just as he told you. It was like a magic trick.

With everything I'd prepared for my presentation, all I had to do was talk from my heart and, at an exciting moment, pull out a prop. Something told me my idea could work. But if, after everything, my pitch didn't go over, I'd still know that Frito-Lay would be missing out on the innovation of the century.

Online Etymology Dictionary, s.v. "authentic (*adj.*)," www.etymonline.com/word/authentic.

FOR YEARS I HAD BEEN PRACTICING BEING THE FUTURE ME BY FINDING occasions to put on the gray suit I'd purchased at Goodwill along with a white long-sleeved button-down shirt. But the one thing I'd never owned was a tie. Even Julius, the sharpest dresser I knew, never wore a tie. What the hell, I thought, if I was going to do this, whether I sailed through it or bombed, I was going to do it looking like a million bucks. So what if the dark blue tie only cost me three dollars at Goodwill? So what if I didn't know how to tie a tie? Well, that probably did matter. Fortunately, my neighbor was a tie expert and tied it for me the night before, loosening it so all I had to do was loop it over my neck and tighten it up.

Early the next morning, after not much sleep, I was showered, shaved, and in my suit when Judy and the boys got up to see me off. With my hundred bags, the transparencies, the fifteen notebooks, and my special prop packaged up, I was ready. Halfway out the door, I paused and then looked back. I'll never forget the pride in my sons' bright eyes, both for me and for themselves because they were part of the operation.

Judy followed me out and, with her understated leadership skills, said a few words that empowered me beyond measure—purely by doing three simple things. First, she *inspired* me. The word *inspire* means to breathe life into another. Second, she *encouraged* me—she took courage and placed it in me on such a deep level that I felt I could stand up to something I'd never really believed I could face. Finally, she *reminded* me of my value and who I was. These are now the three things I try to do to this day to empower my audiences.

Judy said, "You're all set. I don't know anyone who has more courage than you, Richard, and you can do this." And finally she *reminded* me, "Don't forget what your dad and your grandpa told you when you first were hired as a janitor about doing it for your name. You are a Montañez. Now go get what's ours."

That empowerment was a booster and a tonic and everything I needed.

No, it did not keep me from having some serious heart pounding when I arrived and saw the room filling up with many of the Frito-Lay who's who in leadership and management. As I quietly set up my things near the podium I confess to having been nervous—almost throwing-up nervous. Yet thinking of Judy's words, I coasted through my stomach's flip-flops and, in the process, it occurred to me that I was going to be in trouble whether my presentation went well or not. Those who resented me for breaking ranks were going to resent me no matter what. Those who would keep an open mind (despite the protocol I broke) would perhaps be influenced. Again, you don't have to influence everyone, just the right ones.

This was where I found my resolve—namely, knowing that this was all going to have been worth it, whatever the outcome. With that mind-set, I found a kind of steel to ground me—just at the moment I spotted the arrival of the CEO, who was escorted by the plant manager and an entourage of chiefs and top executives. Roger Enrico was a larger-than-life handsome and charismatic figure. Just observing him from a distance as he made the rounds, shaking hands and smiling while also observing everyone, I could see how he commanded the respect that he did—like a general inspecting his troops. He had the manner of making everyone seem important, as if he was in no hurry—even if he was. How did he do that?

Most of the one hundred people present (plus overflow) were our leading executives, and as long as the CEO wasn't looking directly at them, they didn't bother to hide how mad they were about being dragged to this presentation. Red-faced, they were fuming, rolling their eyes, folding their arms, shaking their heads, and occasionally glaring at me.

Later, I'd understand that when the CEO circulated his video to every department, he might have been expecting his highest-ranking executives to think like owners and deliver big ideas. Whatever the outcome of this exercise was going to be, Roger Enrico would be schooling everyone—the janitor beat you all to the punch.

Right before the last of the high-level executives took their seats, a manager finally introduced me to the CEO. The plant manager interjected, "Richard will be making the presentation today," a remark that seemed to surprise Roger Enrico. Nonetheless, he shook my hand, patted me on the back, and reassured me that he was excited about finding out more.

"Thanks for making the trip," I replied and watched him

take his seat in the front row. With that, I signaled to a small squad of my coworkers from production who helped me hand out bags of Flamin' Hots. This gave me a chance to see who was in the room.

Neither Julius nor my other mentor was there, unfortunately, and most likely it was because someone, identity unknown, intended for the audience to be chilly to me. Otherwise the CEO had called in all the big dogs and, for many of them, this was the first time they'd all been together during their tenure. From Dallas there was the chief marketing officer and the president and vice president of sales; from the West Coast division there was the chief operating officer and the chief personnel officer; and from California there were presidents and vice presidents of marketing, sales, and operations. There was also a handful of food scientists from R & D in Texas—familiar faces who had come out to work with me after I'd sent packages of lime and chili seasoning as suggestions.

Apparently, nobody wanted to sample the Flamin' Hot Cheetos—that is, until the CEO nudged others to try them. Reactions were mixed. Staff holding cold cans of Pepsi to pass around were standing along the sides of the room as hands shot up to reach for beverages, and various comments could be heard. Everything from—"Whoa, those are *hot!*" to "Not bad" to "Not enough cheese" to "They're good—but a little red devil on the bag, who came up with that?"

Without further ado, the director of the plant, a notch above the manager, went up to the podium and welcomed everyone, starting with Pepsi-Cola CEO Roger Enrico and moving down the line to the top twelve bigwigs. One of my coworkers delivered a notebook to each of them.

The director thanked everyone for coming and then looked at me, standing below the stage. Was this my cue? I hesitated. There were an uncertain couple of beats where everyone stopped crunching on their samples and waited. "Come on up, Richard," the director said, "you're on."

Everything moved into slow motion, almost like in a dream where you're on stage and forgot to put on your pants or you don't know your lines. My inner voice told me, "Just don't pass out." But miraculously, the minute I got up to the stage, something came over me. Without thinking too hard, I decided that if I moved around like a stand-up comedian or a preacher, it would relax me. And so I grabbed the mic out of the stand and started talking, and walking all over the stage. If I hadn't already been a man of faith, that day would have converted me. Somehow, in the most sincere and beautiful way possible, I tuned out every drop of negativity and God blessed me with the ability to find my voice. Soon I took charge with passion, belief in myself, and, most of all, what I called an answer to the challenge put to all of us from the CEO.

When you believe in yourself, wow, it's life changing. Judy's words were in my ears. She believed in me and I believed in me. So being as authentic as I knew how, I told the story of wanting to make a difference for me and my family and my coworkers. I told about going out with the sales rep to the market in the Hispanic community and seeing that we had no snacks with spice or heat with special appeal to Latinos, no product to target this important market. That was my warm-up to finding a solution, and I had them. They were in suspense. They grasped the need.

But before going further I went to the projector, turned it on, and began my formal presentation. Feeling so professional, I lowered the lights and watched in horror as the transparency appeared upside down. Laughing, improvising a joke, I tried again, only this time the projector threw the image off to the side. Was technology going to derail me?

Finally, it self-corrected and I segued into the theme of how Frito-Lay was missing out on this vibrant culture and the party that went along with it. Then I switched on the lights and went back to storytelling by recalling the day I found the answer and the inspiration for Flamin' Hots. With that, I reached under the podium and pulled out a steaming hot, aroma-rich *elote* with all the trimmings and took a big bite out of it.

"In my neighborhood you can get two of these and put the works on them for two dollars and you've got a meal." Then I took another bite. "I just figured out how to turn a meal into a snack!"

The room erupted into laughter.

So now I was home free, pointing out how roasted corn looked like a Cheeto and how that had been my inspiration for creating the prototype, designing the logo and the bags, and circulating the samples for taste testing. By the time I wrapped up with the rest of the transparencies on the overhead projector, going over the anticipated cost of production, projected revenues compared with some of our more niche products, and reviewing ideas for spin-offs in different strengths of heat and spice, there was a festive atmosphere in the room that couldn't be denied. So much so that I predicted the fiesta in the Latino neighborhood would include mainstream consumers.

Had I been ridiculous? Absolutely! But, once again, greatness sometimes comes in ridiculous forms. When I looked over at the CEO, he had a thoughtful expression on his face that didn't show approval or rejection.

To me, it didn't matter because I had scaled a rock wall, and was about to pull myself up to the next landing. If this was it and was all that would come of my revelation, then something bigger would come along. In the meantime, just as I thanked everybody, and heard polite applause in response as I was about to leave the stage, one of the senior marketing executives shot his hand up.

"Richard," he said in a stern tone, "I just have one question."

I froze for a split second but came back fast, "Sorry, sir, we don't have time for questions." The voice in my brain started to freak out—*Questions? Nobody said anything about questions!*

The marketing executive ignored me completely. He stood right up and challenged me, saying, "This is simple. How much market share are we talking about?"

All the air fled my body. The question sounded like it was in ancient Aramaic. I literally almost fainted. My brain twisted itself up into a pretzel and freaked out some more—*What is market share? I didn't read that chapter!*

But instead of passing out or trying to make up a number,

the fighter in me refused to be intimidated, and the innovator in me decided to answer creatively. Spreading my arms wide, as wide as they would go, I said, with the most audacious smile on my face, "This much market share—that's how much!"

The room went dead silent. You could hear a pin drop. Except then I heard a little giggle. Not too loud. And someone whispered, "Did he say, 'This much market share'?"

Then everything froze and as I stood there with that grin on my face and my arms still spread, I had no idea what to expect next. In that moment Roger Enrico stood up with an "I told you so" look on his face. He turned to the room and said, "Ladies and gentlemen, do you realize that Richard just showed us how to go after this much market share?" And he, too, opened up his arms as far as they could go and smiled even bigger than I had.

THERE YOU HAVE IT, THE FLAMIN' HOT SALES PITCH THAT GAVE ME THE green light to move forward. Not everything was smooth sailing, but one thing was for sure: somehow I had withstood this test of fire. So can you—whether it's for a big presentation or a more modest proposal for a suggestion like an improvement or innovation at work, or for an idea that requires you to get the powers that be to sign on to your project. Obviously, not all pitches and marketing plans need to be so developed. Still, the storytelling rules apply no matter what, for example:

* *The elevator pitch.* This is helpful for many professions. Let's say you got in on the ground floor of an insurance business and you want to go out and get clients. You overhear someone in the elevator talking about needing office insurance and now you have a minute to tell your story. All you need to say is that you are so excited about the services your company offers, mention a USP that makes your approach unique, hand over your card, and say that you're happy to be of help. Your goal isn't to make a sale but to land a potential client. As you walk out the door with that person, get some personal information, then laugh because it's the wrong floor, and say, "Can't wait to hear from you." You will score points for not being too pushy.
* *Let the buyer close the deal.* I love cars. Classic cars, trucks, and motorcycles, too, which have long been my weakness. (Right now I've got some custom classic and sports cars, and a recently acquired Harley.) So when I buy a car from a dealer or at a car show, I don't need a hard sell. The best car salesman I ever met was smart because he figured out that basically I was going to ask questions, and he was going to answer them. Instead, he told me about himself and his family, asked about me and mine, and then let me close the deal. All heart and being authentic. There are some people who need a little pushing, but he was practicing the sales rule of "Know your audience."

* *Present with a partner.* Sometimes when you are telling a decision maker about your project idea, you actually are selling that buyer a compelling story. How? For example, in the entertainment business when you want to pitch a story to a producer—who is making phone calls and has no attention span and only took the meeting as a favor—you have to use shock and awe. The trick that a lot of up-and-coming writers and show creators use is to go in and pitch with a partner, taking turns and trading off storytelling, one of you being funny, the other being dramatic. You can always get a coworker to join you when you are pitching your bosses an idea for the company that already employs you. Bring props.

The more years I've been around the most successful sales and marketing executives, the more I've witnessed one ingredient that will outsell all the others, and that's passion. Bring your heart into a room, know your product or your concept, and put it out there. Passion will always score you extra points even when you don't have the answers to every question. Once you've been given your green light, it's also passion that's going to take you to the next steps of making things happen.

8

When They Come for You, Change Your Game

You did it! You and your flamin' hot self survived the perilous heights and that straight-up rock wall you had to scale. You overcame your worst fears and even allowed yourself to appear or sound ridiculous. You acted like an owner, all the while facing a chorus of *No!* and *Who do you think you are?* After finally being given a resounding *Yes!* you may feel ecstatic—as if you've reached a major pinnacle. Maybe you successfully pitched an idea to your employer, received a raise and a promotion, graduated from a tough academic or training program, opened your own business, got a thumbs-up on or an investment in your start-up, invented a profitable product or service, or discovered a treatment for a serious disease—you name it.

Steel yourself because there is a plot twist coming up you might not have expected.

When you finally pull yourself up to the top and you're standing there, exhausted but proud, you look around and see something you could not have imagined when you started out down at base camp. There's a whole other mountain you still have to climb, twice as high and much steeper than the one you just conquered.

Yes, there are bigger challenges up ahead. You're about to face dangerous terrain and adversaries you never anticipated. Remember all the people and forces we've been discussing who want to steal your destiny? Well, the higher you climb, the more of a leader you become, the more they're going to come after you.

For instance, let's say that you had a taste of success after pitching a cost-cutting measure that has saved your department money. Everyone's impressed—they didn't know you had it in you. But instead of welcoming you to the team that's responsible for taking the idea to the next phase, suddenly a posse of imitators, detractors, and thieves will do all they can to block your path. In the corporate world, backstabbers are notorious. They'll claim credit and try not to give it to you even if it was your revelation. When you start to get the recognition you deserve, they'll rush in to take that away too.

And I know that's probably not the news you were expecting to hear. Sorry, but it's the reality for each of us who dares to go full flamin' hot. In reaching upward to create real opportunities for ourselves, our families, our coworkers, and others, we can expect someone or a few someones out there to try to knock us down.

The good news is that you're about to become a master at

adapting your approach. You can take what you know, mix it up, and move forward with that much more speed, strength, and stamina. All the while you'll be staying one step ahead of anyone trying to throw you off your footing. Just remember—*when they come for you, change your game.*

As we continue, I'll be pointing out three actionable tactics I had to learn:

1. How to detect sabotage.
2. How to stay cool.
3. How to leap into problem-solving mode.

Adaptation, as you'll find, is in your DNA. Know that, and also know that forewarned is forearmed.

AT FIRST I DID NOT SEE *THEM* COMING. IN FACT, IN THAT VICTORIOUS moment when Roger Enrico lit up the room by saying that I had just shown everyone how to go after "that much market share" and then spread his arms out wide, I had never felt so validated in my life.

Amazed, I looked around at the same people who had been so guarded and mad about being there, and I saw change. Sure, they had loosened up a little with me, but as soon as Roger spoke, I saw the lights turn on in their eyes and watched them break out into excited smiles as they nodded their heads.

There was so much freedom in that packed room that I felt like we'd been at a revival. Next thing I knew, after the meeting was called to an end, clusters of conversations started up between the R & D folks, the food scientists, and the sales and marketing people. There wasn't much I could overhear, but everyone, it seemed, was ready to go to work and get Flamin' Hot Cheetos into production.

Roger Enrico made sure I knew that he was there to help at any time and that I had special access to him. But it was also clear that the usual process for launching a new product was now going to be set into motion. There were some congratulations and exclamations of "Good job!" but nobody followed up with any raises or promotions. That was a slight letdown, but I wasn't thinking about credit or compensation. Somewhat naively, I was just happy to be accepted, a player on the team. Obviously, I wasn't going to be in charge of the team, although I did expect to have an important role.

Man, was I wrong! The R & D executives and the food scientists notified me that they were going to bring out Flamin' Hot Cheetos with a seasoning mix that was proprietary and possibly a tiny bit less hot than Judy's original secret sauce. Otherwise, it was a match. They did check with me for taste tests now and then just to see if the flavor retained its appeal and authenticity. I gave them a thumbs-up, assuming that the other strengths of heat would come later.

In the meantime, when I didn't hear anything from the marketing division in Dallas, I checked in with a regional marketing director to ask where things were with the product launch, and he more or less shined me on, suggesting he didn't see me as a leader. "Oh, Richard," he said, "that's not your thing. You're an idea guy and you should stick to that. You don't know anything about strategy."

Strategy? What was he talking about? Frankly, I didn't know what the word even meant. When I looked it up—here's basically what I found:

> A strategy is a broad and general approach to an enter-prise in which certain *structural elements* are deter-mined in advance and *courses of action* have been selected from among others by preference in order to *differentiate* this enterprise from others in light of the *environment* as it is perceived to be and the anticipated action of *opponents* in particular.*

Wordy, but it didn't sound so difficult. When I thought about it, my strategies had led to the achievement of several goals already. Having the vision to see the unseen—what had always been there but had gone unseen until it was revealed—was the idea part, yes. But I'd been practicing how to be stra-tegic in turning those revelations into products and projects with my own R & D company at home all this time.

A little bruised, I figured that I'd go ahead and start put-ting together ideas for future products under the umbrella of Flamin' Hot, among others. Out of more than a dozen inno-vations and policies I created or helped develop and propose,

---

*"Strategy," *Inc.*, updated January 5, 2021, www.inc.com/encyclopedia /strategy.html.

several came from that one Hot franchise, including Flamin' Hot Popcorn, Flamin' Hot Fritos, and Lime and Chile Fritos. While new ideas were in process, I did hear from Dallas that they could use my help.

Over the moon, I rushed home to tell Judy that I'd been contacted by the secretary who worked for one of the lead Frito-Lay food scientist PhDs at HQ, the head of R & D (who had refused to travel to California for the presentation in Rancho Cucamonga). She informed me that her boss, Dr. H. (as I'll refer to him), wanted to meet with me. His department would have me fly out to Dallas—my first time in a plane—to meet with the team. We were so excited. The family and I celebrated in anticipation of all the success to come.

This trip was controversial for starters because I was still an hourly worker, not on salary with travel expenses or any of those perks. Eventually my travel was approved and paid for, and I was told to keep track of my hours—a practice that would last for years. Sometime later I did get an actual promotion to a new position with a title: product packaging manager. Even then I would remain an hourly worker until another controversy erupted.

Standing outside of the Research & Development building in the Frito-Lay headquarters complex in Plano, Texas—twenty minutes north of downtown Dallas—I had the feeling of stepping onto the threshold of my future. Could I see myself as an executive arriving here every day—in this elegant parklike setting? Why not?

My heart beating with excitement, I approached the main check-in desk and gave the receptionist my name.

"Welcome, Mr. Montañez, give me one minute, and I'll get a translator."

I laughed and said, "I speak English."

Apparently, she thought I was an executive from our Mexico division. As one of the first Latino employees to be flown in as a special visitor and walk through the doors there, I could see that she'd just assumed I had to be from another country. She apologized but I said not to worry and then asked if I was in the right place to meet with the head of R & D. Without thinking, I called him Mr. H.

She looked at me in horror. "*Dr. H.,*" she said emphatically. "We only refer to him as *Doctor.*" Under no circumstances would I be allowed to call him by his first name or to call him Mister instead of Doctor. Seemed over the top to me, but he was a senior vice president of Frito-Lay, and I certainly didn't want to be disrespectful.

Finally, I was ushered into his large suite of offices and was again told by his personal secretary to make sure to address him as *Dr. H.* When she then led me into his inner office, there was the burly Scotsman Dr. H. sitting behind his desk like a Scottish general missing only his kilt (which he was known to wear on special occasions). He had a pronounced Scottish accent and a loud voice.

Before I could say a word, he looked me up and down and said, "Oh, you're Richard Montañez."

"Good to meet you, Doctor," I said, and comfortably shook hands with him before taking a seat.

Dr. H. was not someone you'd call an overly warm or pleasant man, but he didn't beat around the bush, which I appreciated.

First, he thanked me for flying out and said, "I just wanted to see how we could work together because you're doing things incorrectly."

This was news to me. What was I doing that was wrong?

"You can't just create a product and expect us to sell something that's not developed correctly. You can't make it up at home and put it in bags and give it out. You'll make people sick." He explained that even in creating prototypes, the water used to soak the corn had to be high-grade with appropriate pH levels. Of course I'd learned that at the plant but didn't bring it up. He had decided to give me a crash course in food science, and I listened attentively.

I told him that this was important information and I would take it into account with future products. Dr. H. wanted to seriously impress upon me that I shouldn't be dabbling in science I knew little about. He showed me around the food labs and introduced me to several of the food scientists and R & D men and women there, some of whom I'd met before. Because I felt confident about my ideas, before I left, I had suggested the possibility of running contests in the future for new snack flavors.

Bad move. Flamin' Hot Cheetos hadn't even been rolled out, so I was probably getting ahead of myself, not thinking for a minute about the possibility of having my destiny stolen.

Yet the more the day wore on and the more PhDs I met, the more I could see that their strategy was to intimidate me. They emphasized their years of schooling and were emphatic about what they could do in the laboratory that I should never attempt on my own. By the time I got home, I couldn't help feeling discouraged, almost as if my brainchild—my creation—had been adopted by strangers who didn't care about its origins. They had taken my revelation, toned it down for mass production, and didn't want my input. There wasn't much I could do, other than maintain my composure and assure everyone that I was just happy to be on the team.

Little could I have guessed at the time of that visit that Dr. H. was behind memos about Flamin' Hot Cheetos that were being sent out to heads of marketing and sales. They read, "Do not support this." Fortunately, those executives also knew that Roger Enrico wanted to see Flamin' Hot Cheetos in the stores.

Also fortunate was the fact that Dr. H. had no leverage when it came to controlling me. That's why he tried to enlist others who could sabotage me.

Unbeknownst to me, Dr. H. went to Al Carey, who now was president of Frito-Lay North America, telling him, "You need to tell Richard to stop."

"No," Al told him, "I can't tell one of my workers to stop thinking." Apparently, they had a heated argument after that.

Later, Al told me about their exchange. Al Carey was not someone to be told what he needed to do. He reassured me, saying, "Don't worry, Richard, keep doing what you're doing. He can't fire you." He laughed and added, "I can because you're on my payroll, but he can't."

His words gave me some relief mixed in with the sting of the reality. The warning signs had been there that I would later not miss. If you ever wonder if you are being sabotaged, here are clues:

* When you've been given a green light and you don't hear any news and then suddenly you do, the power person or people are keeping you off-balance. That's what they do to maintain power.
* If you detect that you are being set up to fail so that you will doubt yourself, that's called gaslighting; if you complain, you may be told you are paranoid.
* When you feel you are being pushed out, you are often still needed for the things you know that they don't. They will push you to the edge but not all the way. That's a clue that you threaten them.

My attitude was to steel myself and take it all in stride. You have to stay cool because (a) haters are gonna hate and you can't change them, (b) you want to avoid stooping to their level, and (c) you might be paranoid. Or so I thought about myself until the time came to actually create product in our plant and R & D sent out a specialist to build the line. Normally such a process takes at least a couple of weeks and a whole team. Sabotage? This time because my plant manager had no budget, the specialist and I had to put together the physical line on our own and then had only four hours to run the product through for the first thousand bags or so. Whatever the specialist set up would give the specifications for producing Flamin' Hot Cheetos on an ongoing basis. Four hours. The specialist from HQ set up a makeshift lab/kitchen, mixed the spices, measured out the cheese, estimated weights and times, and did all the math, checking with me and carefully triple-checking his calculations. We then brought in a skeleton crew for the maiden voyage of my very own revelation.

The first few Cheetos that came off the line looked amazing. They tasted only so-so. They were almost bland. When I said something, he shrugged, saying this was all in exact proportion to how I had first made them at home. Something didn't seem right. The flavor was off. Not sure what to do, I swallowed my concern but felt sick inside. The crew knew nothing. All my friends were high-fiving me and backslapping each other, excited to have been on the first ride. By then, I began to question my concern. Maybe I was overreacting.

That night, while tossing and turning, I received a phone call from the production specialist. He was calling from his motel to say that I was right. He had reviewed his calculations and measurements and found his mistake. When he inputted the ratio of spicy seasoning to Cheeto, he had allotted only half the seasoning per Cheeto. Over the phone, he gave me the specs as they should be. From his tone, I couldn't tell whether he had intentionally made the mistake and his conscience had gotten to him *or* whether it was an honest mistake that he had caught. Whatever the answer, I would never know. All I knew was that I had to find a solution.

So as soon as I hung up with him, I called a handful of my coworkers and asked if they'd come in to help me run the line.

It was the middle of the night and everyone was asleep.

They said yes. They thought I meant the following day. When I explained that we had to do it now, at two in the morning, they all paused, yawned, and then said, "You got it."

None of my crew got paid for that shift. But sometimes you don't do things for money. You do it for your legacy, for history, and for your family. Each of them could claim from then on to have been in the room when the first batch of Flamin' Hot Cheetos was born. They tasted fantastic. Better than I could have ever dreamed.

As before, staying in problem-solving mode had kept me from allowing my destiny to be stolen. From then on, I kept my eyes open, stayed cool, and was ready to get involved— quietly—at a moment's notice.

We now had the means to make the product. The real test, to go out and gain market share, was ahead of us. The regional marketing and sales managers decided against a big launch with advertising or any kind of major promotion. Instead, they chose to introduce Flamin' Hot Cheetos on a limited basis in and around Los Angeles.

This all seemed like a questionable strategy to me, but they had convinced me that they knew what was best, so I didn't worry. They had product, and I assumed everything was moving forward. Another couple of months went by, and then I heard through the grapevine that they were going to ax Flamin' Hot Cheetos.

When I inquired as to whether this was true, some of the less senior marketing people said it was a good try, but unless a product has the potential to earn at least $30 million a year, they phase it out quickly.

Julius had warned me a scenario like this could happen, but I'd refused to believe him. He, too, had hoped word of mouth about Flamin' Hot Cheetos would overcome the lack of support. He had seen the memos that had gone out (all apparently unbeknownst to Roger Enrico), specifically stating not to help me.

Julius could see me getting angry and tried to talk me down. What was I going to do, he asked me, quit? I thought about it and realized that would put me out of a job and not be in anyone's best interests. But after all that Roger Enrico had done to show his belief in me, I couldn't go to him to complain.

It was then that I had a strategic revelation that led to a different kind of approach. The old me had been a fighter with an occasional flamin' hot temper. Now, with everyone fighting me, I had to respond. So if a fight's what they wanted, they would hear from me. But not like in the past. It seemed to me that sometimes the best thing you can do in a fight is not fight. Not outwardly. In so doing, you change your game, you disarm people who think they can get to you. You make yourself unhittable.

If I was going to continue to act like an owner, I was going to have to reject the opinions of those who didn't think I had it in me to maneuver around their strategies with smarter ones of my own. The moral of my new approach was that *it's not how smart you are but how you are smart.*

In this instance, once again, being from the barrio, and having some street cred, was going to give me the adaptive skills I needed right away.

WHEN I SAY IT'S IMPORTANT TO STAY IN PROBLEM-SOLVING MODE, I mean prepare for the backstabbing and develop a mantra—about outsmarting the opposition—to help you avoid taking it personally, even if that is how it's intended. How do you stay cool when you're all churned up inside? Wear sunglasses. Don't let them see you sweat.

When I adapted my reaction, instead of focusing only on the knives in my back, I had to be like a scientist searching for the truth about what was really happening to sabotage a fledgling product. Specifically, I had to get out into the neighborhoods where they were supposedly stocking Flamin' Hot Cheetos in stores but where, I was told, they weren't selling them.

What I found was shocking. Of course, there was no product getting to consumers because the company wasn't putting it out there. By this time, I knew almost all the regular salespeople who delivered orders throughout most of the greater Los Angeles area. And they showed me their numbers to prove it. Sales and marketing weren't promoting the product, so the numbers were bad and there were no reorders.

Even the salespeople were surprised. They loved Flamin' Hot Cheetos but they didn't have any control other than shipping to the addresses given to them. My friend Bill, in sales, tried to comfort me, saying, "It's too bad and you did great. That's how it goes sometimes."

Something didn't add up. If any company knew how to launch a new brand, it was Frito-Lay. Even if they wanted to sideline me, they had to give the "Hots" some kind of a chance.

The next weekend, the family and I drove out to some of the stores on Bill's route, and I immediately saw the problem. There in the rack with all the other familiar products was one bag of Flamin' Hot Cheetos. One bag. Even if someone bought the one bag and loved it, that wasn't enough to give the owners or store managers any big reason to reorder.

My choice was to be furious or counterpunch. What could I do to make a difference? Using my street entrepreneurial skills, I came up with a radical grassroots strategy and emptied out my bank account to put it into motion. First, I mapped out all the little stores and markets that had been shipped the one bag and began to hit as many as possible with the family. We'd go in, buy the one bag, eat it up right in the store, and react with a lot of passion, and I'd approach a manager or owner and ask, "Oh, what are these Flamin' Hot Cheetos? They're great. My kids love 'em. Got any more?"

The clerks, managers, or owners would invariably say, "No, we're out but we'll order more. Come back next weekend." And we would, buying the three or four bags that had been shipped to the store. Pretty soon, we'd come back and see owners and managers with their own stash.

In no time, orders started to multiply exponentially. My strategy worked so well, I hired friends to do the same with their kids. Besides giving them money for the Flamin' Hot Cheetos, I paid them or took them to lunch in return for helping us to cover every store in every Latino neighborhood we could reach. Sales and marketing heads were mystified. Innocently, I'd check in and ask, "You guys still going to ax Hot Cheetos?" and they'd say, "Well, we're getting orders so not yet."

For one month, every Saturday and Sunday, my family and a group of other families did this consistently until mom and-pop grocery stores, 7-Elevens, liquor stores, and bigger super-markets began filling up whole racks of Flamin' Hot product. From almost no business, the orders were coming in at $2,000 a week to $10,000 and higher, escalating from there.

This was only the beginning. Market share improved, but I had to use my vision and my hunger to overcome fears of go-ing broke from my personal efforts to build a customer base in the hood around SoCal. It struck me that any company in-tent on building a loyal customer base for any new product would give away samples. My idea was to do that (without the company footing the cost of it) but in a demographic that would really appreciate the giveaway. Once again I went to Bill in sales, and I asked if he could front me a hundred cases of product. The record keeping allowed him to pick up the tab for just these purposes, so he went for it—until such time as I would be able to pay him back.

My next stop was to pay a visit to an auxiliary bishop of the Roman Catholic Archdiocese of Los Angeles. Respectfully, I asked if we could donate ten cases of Flamin' Hot Cheetos for his parishioners to enjoy after Sunday mass.

"Donate?" He was surprised. Many charitable donations

of food were offered but not usually from the makers of the latest snacks. The auxiliary bishop thanked me profusely, noting that there were many in his flock who were very poor and hungry, and that these snacks would be much enjoyed. His excellency himself took a bag from me and immediately became a fan.

After mass on the first Sunday we did this, I was so happy to see families like mine eager to open up their bags of Flamin' Hot Cheetos, devour them, and immediately ask (at least by those who could afford occasional snacks), "Where can we buy more of these?"

The flavor of the chili actually does have a mild warming effect that's very pleasant for taste buds, while the touch of sugar offsets the spice and makes you want more. When we did this the first time and later at other churches in the archdiocese, we'd get the names of the neighborhood stores and hurry to these spots to fill out orders. The beneficiaries of this strategy were not just Flamin' Hot Cheetos and Frito-Lay but also all the shops and markets whose business would also be improved. I didn't know it at the time, but as a future executive, I was developing a model for community development and strategic alignment with retail partners that no one in those days had done in the same way. For instance, if a charity came to Frito-Lay asking for a check to support an upcoming fundraiser, I would partner with a local business that sold our products (such as a grocery store chain)—get the check written out from our community development fund and give it to that business, and have them cosponsor the event or program by buying a table at the fundraiser or putting up signage. Why not spread good will all around? Why not advance the Flamin' Hot and other PepsiCo brands *and* our retail partners across communities?

From as far back as I could recall, even in my hungriest days, I had always known there was someone else hungrier and poorer than me who could be given a part of what I had to eat. At the time that I was emptying my bank account to save Flamin' Hot Cheetos from being dumped into the spicy-snack dustbin of history, I was hungrier than ever. So I could relate to the families who were so surprised and happy to be handed a fun free snack on their way out of church. This street marketing was actually a gift. It made me happy to get out and around Los Angeles, help spread the word, build a customer base, and offer something free to those who couldn't afford to buy their own bag.

We did that for a month, and the area stores sparked a serious buzz. At Frito-Lay headquarters, nobody could figure out where this momentum had come from—with no marketing dollars, no advertising. All they knew was that they couldn't cancel Flamin' Hot Cheetos as long as there were orders. At least not yet.

One night in talking to Judy about customers I wanted to reach, she asked me, "Who are the best food shoppers?"

That was easy. "Homemakers, of course," I answered.

She agreed. Most household budgets were created and enforced by moms, wives, and working women. If you had a limited budget, what would make you prioritize a spicy snack? Obviously, you'd have to love the snack and have it feel like a party or other special occasion when you opened up a bag.

As I thought about her questions, I remembered that we had a friend who was very high up in a local Tupperware group. When I called her and asked if she'd like free product for her meetings, she was thrilled. After I delivered several cases to her, she couldn't wait to tell me how all the ladies fell in love with Flamin' Hot Cheetos and were all rushing out to their local stores to make sure they had lots in stock. With word of mouth, these Tupperware ladies—homemakers, moms, and others who made up the number one category of shoppers—became an unpaid sales force talking up a Frito-Lay product to their counterparts nationwide.

The resource of adaptation had served me well. Not many months earlier I hadn't had a clue what *market share* even meant. Within a few months I was paving the way for my eventual calling card as the Godfather of Latino Branding!

With all of this increase in business, our hours did go up at the plant, and I was confident that the hard climbing of this next phase was over. I couldn't have been more wrong.

Despite an increase in demand coming from Latino neighborhoods across Southern California, it appeared that the decision makers had decided that the test-marketing phase was over. Once again I heard that the numbers, though promising, weren't big enough. For all this time I had avoided complaining to Roger Enrico or Al Carey. But finally I had to say something to make sure they understood that there had been

no marketing help or budget whatsoever and we had still begun to capture that important demographic and market
share I'd promised.

In a matter of hours, one of the top marketing executives
was on his way to Los Angeles to work with me. When I
showed him what had been achieved without any help, he
shrugged it off. His reaction could not have been more racist.

"Are you telling me that Frito-Lay doesn't care about
Latino culture and consumers?" I asked, pushing back for a
change.

"Not at all," he corrected me. He knew that the Hispanic
population was growing, and he valued this new group of
customers. But then he showed me numbers. Only 2 percent
of the snack business was made up of consumers who were
Latino. For a product to have a long shelf life, we had to go
after that other 98 percent of all potential buyers.

All at once the smoke cleared. I didn't have to be mad or
take his seeming disrespect for my people too personally. In
fact, I was grateful. He had given me vital information. So
then I told him what I'd been doing in the Latino neighborhoods, and he not only gave me my props but said he'd request at least a modest budget so that I could keep doing the
same thing but in other demographics too.

And that's what happened. With a few more dollars and
a chance to legitimately work on marketing, I did exactly
the same thing in the African American community that
I'd done in my own hood. Julius encouraged me and helped.
The family and I went back and visited the stores in those

communities and got to know the owners and managers. Then we started giving out samples after church services, and several Black pastors became some of my best and lasting friends. We donated Flamin' Hot Cheetos to more Tupperware groups and other women's organizations.

Julius and I used to laugh about the fact that both Latinos and African Americans were already putting hot sauce on their chips—right into the bags—before Flamin' Hot Cheetos came along. In any event, once we went national with an official launch, we were set up to be a hit in every hood. Instead of having to go across the tracks to introduce mainstream consumers to Hot Cheetos, they crossed over to us, not wanting to miss out on the new favorite flavor of urban America.

By the early 1990s, Flamin' Hot Cheetos were officially a staple of the Frito-Lay family of brands, on our way to becoming a multibillion-dollar-a-year brand.

This didn't mean that my earlier detractors weren't still trying to come after me, unfortunately. There were still more big lessons to learn.

BY 1995, AGAINST ALL ODDS, FLAMIN' HOT CHEETOS WAS NO LONGER IN danger of being dropped. My reputation as an idea person who could also do strategy was improving, even though the destiny thieves were always at the ready to block me. Most of the time

I accepted that higher-level managers and executives were going to resent any potential of my surpassing them in terms of accomplishment and access to senior and top-level executives. The one thing I couldn't tolerate was when it was my ethnicity that set them off. The fact is, systemic racism was rampant, and it continually raised its head, though usually in insensitive remarks, not outright slurs.

One executive in particular, JT—a top production guy, well-respected for running successful divisions and product campaigns, also known for making racist and sexist remarks—had misunderstood a comment I had made about him and decided to come after me. The comment was a compliment about how good he was at his job, but the way it was relayed somehow implied that I wanted his job. Not the case at all, but it added to how threatened by me he'd always acted.

JT had been very comfortable with the old command and control system that by the mid-1990s had certainly changed under the leadership and influence of Roger Enrico. By that point, Roger had adapted many of the antiquated ways of doing business that had become bad habits at Frito-Lay. He had cut overhead and operational costs, not to everyone's liking, and had gone after the way that managers spent too much money on their own perks and not enough on training programs and incentivizing excellence in job performance. Across the company, 1,700 employees were let go and many of those were managers who didn't fulfill meaningful functions. After asking all of us to act like owners, Roger assured those of us who didn't get cut that the savings wouldn't go to executive pay but instead toward creating more hours and opportunity for growth for frontline workers.

Executives like JT hated that change and, apparently, that made him resent me all the more because he knew that I had Roger Enrico's ear and his trust. This was news to me, however, until it all came to a head at a conference I'd been invited to attend in Dallas about new kinds of machinery we were adopting in all of our plants. Because I was the guy who had written training manuals and overseen training, it was only natural that I'd be included at the conference—to demonstrate the new packaging machine that was going to improve the work process at a lot of the plants.

At one point, I saw JT walking toward me as if he were on the warpath. Asking to talk to me, he pulled me out into the hallway of the large conference center and blasted away, cussing me out—about how I'd f—d up this and blank-blanked that, and who did I think I was? "And I don't care if you are Mexican or if Roger Enrico is Mexican. . . ." Most people knew very well that Enrico was Italian American, but I didn't correct JT. Instead, I just looked at him without giving away how upset I was. He ranted and raved about my efforts to diversify our product line that were hurting his bottom line.

His finger in my face, he said, "I am going to make your life miserable, and you can count on that." There were some slurs and more four-letter words thrown in there too.

Rather than react in a way that would jeopardize my future (my instincts were to punch him in the face, but I held my tongue and my fists), I wound up taking the problem to Roger Enrico during a trip to PepsiCo headquarters in New

York. It was rare for me to complain to the CEO about mistreatment by an executive. I come from a world where you don't snitch, even if it's about someone who has it in for you. But I had my limits.

Roger's advice was wise. He said, "Richard, I could pick up the phone, make one call, and he'll be gone." Sounded good to me, but Roger continued, "Or you can fix this, and I'll tell you how."

Resolved to take care of business myself, I listened as Roger gave me guidance that can be applied to many situations. He said that he had been forced to learn to change himself rather than try to change others, and that way he avoided letting his detractors throw him off his purpose. In earlier days he said he had learned a lesson about handling a problem without causing a conflict that created more of a problem. There was a culture of men going to strip clubs after work, and he saw the impact that it had, indirectly, on how women were treated on the job. Instead of forbidding them to go or being combative and critical, Roger changed himself and made it known that he would no longer be participating in those outings to those clubs. He started to propose other outings after work that didn't involve situations that objectified women. Changing himself and how he led others had a ripple effect on the culture of the company, which began promoting more women to positions traditionally held by men.

It was clear to me that JT was never going to change. If I was going to change instead, I had to do something besides allowing myself to be humiliated. Somehow I had to find a way to change myself yet still stand up to him—without resorting to the street fighter side of me. Roger observed that there were grounds for JT to be let go. But if I gave the signal for him to be fired, there would be others who would come after me just as hard. Or, Roger suggested, "you could address the problem yourself. You can ask him to apologize. You can go to HR and have them facilitate an apology. But the request is coming from you."

I had never gone to HR to complain about anyone. That alone was a huge leap. Again, reporting someone to the authorities, where I come from, can be seen as kind of lame. Weak. My attitude was wrong. Human resource departments are supposed to keep complaints confidential and handle conflicts quietly and by the book. Sometimes you need that. In my case, it helped, and required a change from me to ask for their intervention.

In hindsight, I realize that legally I could have filed a major complaint, even a lawsuit. That wasn't true to my values. So when I reported JT to HR, I made it clear that I didn't want to get him fired; I only wanted an apology and to make sure it never happened again to me or to anyone else. They flew him out to California and put him up at a hotel, allowing him to deliver his half-hearted apology in person to me but without the audience of others I wished could have been there to hear him. That being said, JT and I never had a problem again. To the best of my knowledge, he was less antagonistic to others in general.

If Roger had fired JT with a phone call or if I had filed a

legal complaint through HR, I might have had a brief moment of seeing him get his comeuppance. But I would not have been able to stay at the company much longer. Even though JT had been in the wrong, I would have been blamed more. Ultimately, I would have lost out.

That's why the end of the story is that sometimes you have to lose a battle to win the war. Once I'd broken ranks and tapped into corporate America as a janitor, a production manager, a community development manager, an executive, and, in time, a vice president of PepsiCo, many of the systemic poisons were no longer tolerated. That's how I won.

The JTs of this world are sent to teach us a lesson so we can choose not to be like them and not to be deterred on the path to our destiny. Whenever possible, we can choose to appreciate the JTs and be happy that we aren't them.

Another lesson I learned is that not everyone really wants to steal your destiny. Other motivations can be at play.

EVERY TIME I PITCHED SOMETHING NEW, I WAS WELL AWARE THAT THE first person I'd hear screaming about it in his Scottish accent would be Dr. H.

I felt secure just to keep doing what I did—because Dr. H. couldn't fire me. The person who could actually fire me was the senior vice president of operations, under whose jurisdiction

I fell. He and I had no problem. From early days, we had been friendly. Then I got the news that he had decided to retire, and guess who was going to replace him?

If you guessed Dr. H., you would be right. My solution was to avoid him, not the hardest thing to do, seeing as I was in California and Dr. H. was in Texas. Suddenly a visit from him was announced on our schedule. He had never been to visit—there was no real reason for it—but now he wanted to come and tour the Rancho Cucamonga plant.

My supervisor approached me the day before Dr. H. was supposed to arrive and said, "Richard, we have some movie tickets we want to give you. For tomorrow. Take the day off. Go to the movies."

"Why?" I asked. I'd never been offered a day off or movie tickets before. Something was fishy.

"Well . . ." The director hemmed and hawed and then told me Dr. H. was coming, and "we don't want you to upset him."

My response was a low-key. "No thanks. I'm not going to do that. I got a job to do."

That put an end to that. The next day Dr. H. came through, and I shook his hand, welcoming him to our plant. No drama, no lectures. Everyone appeared to be relieved.

A little more than two months later, I was invited to attend a major weeklong sales rally and conference for Frito-Lay in a Dallas hotel. Flamin' Hot Cheetos were doing phenomenally well, but I wasn't involved with sales and marketing for the brand so I didn't understand why the invitation had come to me. Nobody could explain why I was included.

Flying out with my plant manager and director made me

nervous. When I arrived, it was clear that the man running the entire thing was Dr. H. It was strange to me that some of the executives and R & D people I knew had asked me to come down to the front row to sit with them.

Dr. H. took to the stage and spoke directly to the sales managers, using a PowerPoint slide show to give them motivational practices and mantras he wanted them to share with their sales teams. He went on: "I want you to tell them they can do this and reach beyond earlier successes. They can do this. But it's important for me to tell you the one thing I don't want you to let them do. I don't want you or anyone on your team to create any new products."

When he said that, I felt my stomach tighten. Had I been brought here to be told off at this huge rally?

Dr. H. went on: "And the reason I don't want you to create new products is because you don't know how to do it." He was yelling at this point.

Sweat had started to pour off my face. My body felt like it was going to melt off my seat and onto the floor. There was only one person in that room I imagined he was addressing. And it was me!

Dying, I looked to my left and spotted a young marketing executive I used to call for advice occasionally and watched as he stood up and spoke, without a mic, but in a very loud voice, saying, "Doctor, I disagree with you!"

The Scotsman's nostrils flared as he looked down at this young marketing executive. "And?"

The young man shot back, "Have you ever heard of a team member named Richard Montañez?"

Dr. H. shook his head, almost with a laugh. He replied, "I know Richard. I know the hundreds of letters I get from Roger Enrico weekly. I know Richard Montañez. What about him?"

The young marketing executive said at the top of his voice, "You know he created a new product. What about an idea like that?"

Dr. H. nodded, shrugged, and glared down at me. Then he turned to look at the screen behind him. All of a sudden it lit up with a chart showing a bag of Flamin' Hot Cheetos. Another slide came up and it showed the latest numbers, how much revenue was being made from all parts of the country. A gasp ran through the ranks. The numbers were epic!

In my state of surprise, it took me a while to realize that all of this had been planned. Dr. H. proceeded to give me the most heartfelt apology. He said that he had been wrong and he was grateful I hadn't listened to him before and that he also had to thank everyone he'd encouraged *not* to help me because they hadn't completely listened either.

There wasn't a dry eye in the house. The handkerchiefs came out as people began to dab at their tears. If that wasn't enough, Dr. H. had created an award for me in my honor that he called the Kick Ass Award—because, as he said in his Scottish clip, "You kicked the Big Ass."

All at once, one thousand or more attendees laughed and began to cheer.

Before I went up to accept the award, Dr. H. took his suit jacket off to reveal a brand-new Flamin' Hot Cheetos T-shirt. He had to say a few more words to all who didn't know the full story. He explained, "I made a judgment that was not correct and tried to discourage Richard, but thankfully I didn't succeed. He taught us all what's possible."

People started to audibly cry. He was barely keeping it together. I was overwhelmed. Dr. H. summoned the chief marketing officer and the president of sales to the stage, saying, "Can you two come up here? I need you to hold me up."

He humbled himself beyond anything I could have imagined. Finally, he said, "Richard Montañez, come up here."

Slowly I walked up to the stage. It had been seven years since I had made my presentation at the plant back home for Roger Enrico. Everything was in slow motion again. All one thousand attendees leaped to their feet, everyone crying and applauding as I walked up to get my award. Dr. H. gave me the mic and I just thanked him and everyone there. It was surreal, humbling, and wonderful.

Some years later at Dr. H.'s retirement party, after we had collaborated on some more creative products and marketing campaigns—including a contest for employees to pitch product ideas—I had a memorable, short conversation with him. He gave me a hearty bear hug and whispered in my ear, "You're an angel. You came into my life when I needed to change. Thank you."

And that's when I realized that changing someone is much the same as influencing them. Likewise, you don't have to change everyone, just the right ones.

While I'm the first to say that you should pay attention to the red flags from competitors who want you to fail, the reason you should keep your cool and not give them any energy is that it keeps you from playing your game, from being the best you that you were always meant to be.

Two strategies can help here: (1) Remember that the best revenge is success. The more they hate, the more you can flourish, the less they can get to you. (2) Forgive them. That's what my spiritual teaching has taught me. There is nothing as powerful as wishing someone well in your heart and spirit who has been unkind.

With my temper, I can't say it's always been easy, but you know that saying about not wanting anyone to live in your psyche rent free? The people who don't have your best interests at heart don't deserve to have you sweat a minute over them.

You might assume that after Flamin' Hot Cheetos was sent into orbit, it was only a hop and a skip until I made it to the boardroom. Not exactly. Yes, the stage had been set, but I hadn't figured out how to learn my lines.

9

Why Words Matter and Other Leadership Lessons

A side from the question about how to have your own hot flamin' breakthrough, the question I'm most often asked is—*Richard, how do you become a leader?*

For many who have risen from entry-level jobs to positions of responsibility or even businesses of their own, this is a critical question: How do you push yourself to go up to the big leagues and make the leap to being truly flamin' hot? My answer is that we all have different leadership styles, and it's up to us to choose what gives us the most impact.

We all have the capacity to lead. While no one is born a leader, we are all born to lead—to lead something, someone, or a lot of someones. And it's not the title that makes the person; rather it's the person who makes the title. That's why, no matter where you are on the totem pole, whether you are unemployed, self-employed, or employed by a company or an institution, leadership comes alive when you begin to become as invested in the success of others as you are in your own success.

You may wonder, *Hmm, what is it that I have to offer as a leader that adds value to the success of others?* Those are questions a lot of us ask even when the answers are right in front of us.

We all have the potential to have a voice and to use it in a purposeful way.

START WITH THE POWER OF YOUR VOICE. OF ALL THE IMPORTANT leadership skills, for me communication is at the top. Call that Leadership Lesson Number One—the need to communicate powerfully. That's why I fell in love with etymology. The process of investigating words is like opening up a treasure chest of history, language, culture, and anthropology.

You don't have to use big Ivy League words or trendy slangy words or appealing catchphrases—unless you feel comfortable playing with language. What matters is that you harness your voice and your beliefs by choosing words that help you describe yourself and your vision to others who in turn can be motivated by them. Words can help you organize your creative insights into shareable information. Words are stealth messengers to the brain that help us speak our revelations into reality.

For example, if you are someone with great ideas but who is constantly saying, "I never can catch a break" or "I don't have any connections," your cells are listening and imprinting the language of "I never can" and "I don't have" on your psyche. The opportunities that you could be creating for yourself tend to vanish when you speak them out of existence. The opportunities float off to linger around someone who knows how to be an opportunity/prosperity whisperer.

In that time period before I had my big revelation to put chili on a Cheeto, I used to talk out loud and declare that my revelation was on its way, coming up around the corner, just out of reach. Little revelations started to happen before the Big One. But even then I told myself so confidently *it* was about to happen, *it* did. That kind of self-talk is a learned skill. Anyone can do it. Similarly, as a leader who wants to empower others, the language of imminent success can supercharge the team. You tell others you expect good things from them and you give them the words to speak to themselves the same way.

In my experience there is a direct correlation between poverty and illiteracy. I've also found that the fastest way to increase your prosperity is to become more literate. The most successful prosperous leaders I've ever met are lifelong learners, intense listeners, and exceptional storytellers. They stay in shape by reading, observing nature, listening to people from different walks of life—and being adventurous in their curiosity.

When I first overcame my fear of looking ridiculous, I became much better at asking people what a word or an expression meant. That in turn sparked my curiosity to know more, and that's how I developed my passion for etymology. The histories of words, their meanings and derivations, are histories of our journeys as human beings. As I improved my vocabulary and my comfort level with using it, I felt more at ease conversing with people who came from backgrounds that should have been intimidating to me but weren't.

One thing I began to notice early on was how some words—slurs, disses, and other kinds of deprecating language—could become triggers for conflict. When I was younger, there were things people would say that I'd be the first to counter with "Those are fighting words!" Later, as I started to probe more deeply into the evolution of words, I was disturbed to find that derogatory views of others were embedded in certain usages of even technical language.

This issue came up in connection with updating the Frito-Lay training manuals in the mid-1980s, and I remember having a conversation about it with a group of our top engineers from across the country that I'd been invited to join—because of my knowledge of all the equipment that I could run and fix. These were highly skilled college-educated engineers, all white and over forty years old, and I was in my late twenties—Latino, with no formal engineering training, and given most of my technical knowledge by my dad, the fix-everything man. As we turned to a chapter that introduced master-slave terminology, I objected. Despite the derogatory implication, aspects of these terms have continued in many kinds of machinery and even digital technology. Basically one device that controls a group of others is known as the master while the devices it controls are the slaves. Currently in the tech world, the term *master-slave controller* endures, with a recent *Wired* magazine article noting, "The words *master* and *slave* have been widely used for decades in computing and other technical contexts, as a reference to situations where one process or entity controls another. Sometimes the metaphor is less precise: A 'master' may simply lead, serve as a primary resource, or be considered first."*

The terminology in mass production had offended me for years and it bothered others who worked as part of my team, so I felt someone had to say something. We were getting ready to move on when I quickly said, "This all needs to be out. We can't talk about a master versus slave."

Every single one of the men in the room was fast to argue. One said, "It's a perfect term. We've been teaching it for years. It's part of our DNA."

"That's the problem," I shot back. "Bad DNA. Time to change it. The term is offensive to many." (Later when I mentioned my stance to one of the few female managers, someone who was often in my corner, she agreed with me.)

The engineers and I went back and forth in our discussion.

---

*Elizabeth Landau, "Tech Confronts Its Use of the Labels 'Master' and 'Slave,'" *Wired*, July 6, 2020, www.wired.com/story/tech-confronts-use -labels-master-slave.

They saw nothing wrong. In fact, in that era, international employees officially referred to plants as plantations—another usage that brings up slavery.

These engineers were technically competent in the extreme, intellectually gifted, but they weren't used to having their lore and language questioned. Carefully, I explained that we had a diverse workforce and that diversity starts with having a DNA everyone can relate to.

That was a personal breakthrough for me—to hold my own with the brainiest guys around, not be intimidated, and have them consider my argument. They gave in and agreed to the terminology change. They even begrudgingly accepted that the change had been overdue.

If you've ever been that person who wished you had said something or if you would like to use your voice even more, I hope it will be helpful for me to recall some of the leadership lessons I learned about speaking up and out. It took me a long time to understand that very often the most powerful words I could summon at a particular moment in time weren't about me but about something important that needed to be said.

Sometimes a challenge will arise that as a leader you'll feel compelled to address, and the words you most need will be right there for you. Trusting that moment is a test of leadership. The trick is to be ready with your lines and prepared for that moment when you recognize—*Oh, the stage has been set and this is my cue!* Sometimes you are ready with what needs to be said and sometimes you're not.

YOU MAY NOT KNOW THIS YET, BUT THE EXAMPLE OF YOUR SUCCESS CAN be the greatest blessing to someone else. It took me a while to recognize this Leadership Lesson Number Two, which many refer to as leading by example. Leaders who show the way simply demonstrate how far they've made it so that you can too.

And that aspect of leadership was in my mind a lot as the 1990s came to a close. After more than twenty years with Frito-Lay, I started to become restless and had begun to consider leaving the company. Though I had been given a couple of promotions, they didn't come with the pay increase of a higher-level manager or the benefits that went along with that kind of job. If my hope was to show others what was possible, maybe it was time to go somewhere where the compensation would be equitable.

Judy was even more frustrated. Whenever I brought up my analogy of climbing the rocks up the mountain, she would say that she saw the challenges differently. Her feeling was that every time I overcame all the shouts of "No!" and "Who do you think you are?" they'd reward me by taking me out on the ocean in a boat and then throw me into the water and leave me, making it my choice to drown or dog-paddle in the stormy seas back to shore. Judy would say, "Richard, you keep figuring out a way to come back and get the job done, but as soon as you get back to shore, they put you in the boat again and throw you in the water even farther out. And you still paddle your way back. You still keep proving that you can take it. But this is getting old."

The thought of going elsewhere wasn't appealing, but that option couldn't be ruled out. Ironically, one of the places where I'd tried to get a job before Frito-Lay was at Pepsi's archrival—Coke. They rejected me, saying they didn't think I could learn to run the technology.

Twenty plus years later I heard that many CEOs were asking, *Where's my janitor? Where are my waste-saving ideas? And training manuals? Where are my Flamin' Hot Cheetos?* Finding a new position wouldn't be that hard. But in my stubbornness, every time I got thrown out of the boat into the ocean, somehow it made me want to fight and swim harder and prove myself even more.

Maybe I should have complained. After the amazing acknowledgment I received from Dr. H., I did expect to receive a promotion. When that didn't happen, I should have used my voice to speak up on my own behalf, but I didn't. My bad— especially because the obvious person whose ear I had would have been Steve Reinemund.

After Roger Enrico took over from Wayne Calloway as CEO at PepsiCo, he brought in Steve to run Frito-Lay (and later, to the surprise of many, as his replacement as CEO of PepsiCo). Some of the ways that Roger had sought to fortify PepsiCo was by bolstering the restaurant acquisitions made earlier, trimming the fat in the different divisions, and creating more cohesion between snacks, beverages, and restaurants. An ex-Marine with supersized energy, Steve Reinemund came to

Frito-Lay after running Pizza Hut successfully and with the full confidence of Roger Enrico, who once said, "Steve is the most effective driver of a business that I've ever seen."

Had I gone to Steve, I would have learned that there had been an offer of a promotion to a managerial position with a raise, improved benefits, and an opportunity to advance. As I later found out, the regional director responsible for bringing me the offer never gave it to me. The director came to see me at work to ask if I was happy—having been told to make sure that I was. My answer was "Yeah, I'm happy. I'm good." Little did I know that would give him the excuse not to give me the offer. It remained in his briefcase.

That part of the story never got back to Steve Reinemund, who assumed that I was happy and being compensated well. Because I didn't know that an offer had been available but never given to me, the thought of leaving the mother ship was easier. If I left, it would be without regret, having benefited from years of unconventional training in executive leadership—because of the access I'd had to all of the corporate executives. Whenever I had a project or innovation to discuss, I usually had the ear of some of the smartest leaders in the business world, including every single CEO of PepsiCo during my tenure. That had begun with my sending letters and ideas to our founder, Don Kendall, who was chairman from 1971 to 1986, and to Wayne Calloway, who was CEO from 1986 to 1995. I was also very close to Al Carey, who became president/CEO of Frito-Lay, and to my great mentor, Roger Enrico, whose tenure as CEO of PepsiCo was from 1995 to 2001. During those years I had direct access to Roger, and from him I received the Chairman's Award, which is given to only one employee within the entire PepsiCo corporation per year and recognizes contribution, leadership, and work ethic that has had a major impact on the company as a whole. The same was true when Roger left in 2001 and I reported to Steve Reinemund, receiving the Chairman's Award from him as well as from his successor, Indra Nooyi, who took over in 2006, remaining at PepsiCo for the rest of my time there, and who also gave me the Chairman's Award. Each of these visionaries revealed different brilliant facets of leadership, and I could write a book on each about their contributions to my leadership journey.

What each of these leaders exemplified in their own right was an appreciation for the fact that the solutions and innovations that most strengthen a company come from the rank and file, even from entry-level and frontline workers. Not every business or company shares that philosophy, but those that do are the most enduring. One of the most famous examples of leadership in problem solving arose from the front line at Sony. Before the advent of the iPod and iTunes, there was a time when the Sony Walkman personal music-playing devices dominated that industry. Sony missed the boat, however, when everything started changing from cassettes and CDs to downloadable music files from the internet. Apple got to that new frontier first and left Sony in the dust.

Overnight, Sony took a nosedive and would have crashed forever had it not been for a leadership that valued input from across their divisions. It turned out that a frontline worker had developed a game and suggested innovating a game system he proposed, which became PlayStation. Today Sony Play-Station is in its fifth edition, and gaming has become a major contributor to Sony's fortunes.

Luckily, I had worked for CEOs who set an example of humility by sharing the belief that leaders can come from above or below. Because of that enlightened approach, I was blessed to be able to develop my own approach to leadership—with systems that were implemented at manufacturing plants and retail chains in this country and around the world, later opening doors for me to lecture halls at top MBA programs. There aren't many settings where a janitor and a CEO could have teamed up to improve the ways executives learn from frontline workers, as well as the other way around.

As a result of my collaboration with Roger Enrico, which was aimed at empowering employees at every level, I was empowered to create a model that would allow workers to remind management of our value to the corporation—with a metric we could use, as in a quantifiable measure for a worker's individual contribution. For example, I started keeping track on a daily basis of how much money I'd saved or made the company that day. I wanted to be able to show that if I earned three hundred dollars that day that my work hours had generated product that would be valued and sold for that amount or more. My productivity would be helping the company's bottom line, not taking away from it.

My formula was aimed at giving myself and my coworkers a sense of our worth in dollars and cents. When the time came to getting a raise and added benefits, the union set those terms. That was fine, but if we really wanted empowered employees, I believed we should still be communicating the ways in which overall profits and growth resulted from every worker's contributions.

Now, the flip side to this empowerment issue was the challenge and responsibility of enlightened leaders to motivate employees over the long haul. Breaking it down, I concluded that there are basically two kinds of leaders—Pharaohs and Deliverers. A Pharaoh, as we know from Scripture and history, is one who takes captives and holds them by force, demanding to be served first. Under a Pharaoh, those who serve have no chance to rise and experience growth. You can recognize a Pharaoh as any number of authoritarians who take people captive to build everything in their image. Everything looks like them and everything is about them.

A Deliverer, in contrast, is one who brings a message of freedom and growth to all who can hear, communicating in words that uplift, and with a strategy of serving others first. Deliverers help people to break out of the bonds and the chains that have held them back. Deliverers are not threatened by diversity or individuality and are more about others than about themselves.

Moses, many of us know, was the original Deliverer, who demanded of Pharaoh, "Let my people go!" His words did what every great leader's words should do—he secured the freedom for his people to move in the direction that they were intended to go. The message today reminds CEOs—let the front line lead. It says to ministers—let the congregation lead. And it tells our legislators—follow the lead of your constituents and let their votes lead.

In speaking up to Pharaoh, Moses had to be careful and direct with his words. It's not that well known, but Moses actually had a speech impediment. Some have interpreted references to it to mean he had a stutter and others have suggested he had a physical disability that made it hard for him to form words. As the Bible tells us, when God first singles out Moses for the job of Deliverer, Moses suggests maybe he's not the right guy. Here's what we learn in Exodus 4:10:

> But Moses said to the Lord, Oh, my Lord, I am not eloquent, either heretofore or since thou has spoken to thy servant; but I am slow of speech and of tongue.

This obviously didn't change the mind of the Lord, who advises Moses not to worry because He will provide the right words for him to use when the time comes—starting with "Let my people go."

In sharing my theories of leadership with you, I assume that you have known both Pharaohs and, hopefully, Deliverers in your encounters in life and at work. My hope is that you'll choose the path of a Deliverer and look to set others free so they can go toward the lives they were intended to live. When you do, trust the Moses model and know that you'll be given the right words at the right time.

Moses's job as a leader and motivator wasn't easy. He had to get everyone to follow him through the desert.

When the words don't come easily, Moses teaches you to rely instead on your spirit of optimism and your ability to energize—even electrify—your listeners. The electrical current can also ignite your imagination and give the words you do use added currency. When you choose, you can actually become an energy conductor of optimism.

A Deliverer is a leader who electrifies followers and lets them know their capabilities. The word *electrify* can refer to a performance or oratory, as this definition shows:

> To charge with electricity, to equip, for use of electric power, to supply with electric power, to amplify . . . to excite intensely or suddenly. . . . Synonyms: charge, excite, exhilarate, galvanize, intoxicate, pump up, thrill, titillate, turn on.*

If the idea seems preposterous that you have within you the ability to lead and electrify others, let's not forget where we began our discussion about *you* and how flamin' hot you can be. Trust, as I had to learn to do, that when the right words are needed, they will come.

AS A LEADER COMMITTED TO DOING THE RIGHT THING, SOMETIMES YOU have to put your reputation on the line to stand up for what is right. We can call this Leadership Lesson Number Three—

---

*Merriam-Webster.com Dictionary, s.v., "electrify (v.)," www.merriam-webster.com/dictionary/electrify.

acting with the courage of your convictions. The reality of that hit me during a memorable experience I had after receiving an unprecedented invitation from Roger Enrico to attend the annual shareholder meeting in Dallas—which wasn't usually held there. This was during the period when I was thinking about leaving, and the thought of attending the meeting itself wasn't something I was dying to do. But Roger usually had a reason for doing things, and as I learned when I got there, he wanted to include me at a dinner and introduce me to some of the members of the board of directors, who became friends over time, and also wanted me to attend a meeting of the board.

Maybe, I thought, it was his way of exposing me to every facet of corporate governance. When the day of the shareholder meeting arrived, I honestly thought some of the customary procedures were somewhat boring, but then it turned out that Roger wanted to give me a special recognition with the board present. When the moment came, he surprised me by saying, "Richard Montañez, please stand up," and then he introduced me as "vice president of everything," which received vigorous applause. He added, "I call him a VP because he thinks like one," and proceeded to commend me for personifying the Frito-Lay/PepsiCo brand and for many accomplishments that exemplify leadership from the front line.

The gesture meant a lot to me and as the presentations and voting matters wrapped up, I found it interesting to observe the long lines of shareholders who had traveled from far and wide to address the board with questions and requests for the coming year.

There was a group of nuns who were extremely pleased with their investment—they owned more than a hundred thousand shares for their retirement—and they just wanted to make sure their money would continue to grow at the same pace in the coming decade. They really had no questions, so they were thanked and waved on. The whole experience was eye-opening in terms of how responsive to shareholders the board and the top executives must be. Then just at the end, an attorney with the Teamsters Union, which invested in PepsiCo stock, came up to the mic. He said he was there not on behalf of the Teamsters but on behalf of all shareholders. His issue, he said to Roger, was: "We're aware that you donated your salary of almost a million dollars last year to a scholarship fund for the children of frontline workers. But what I want to know is what you are going to do with the rest of your compensation package. You have not told us about your plans for your stock options or your annual bonus of over a million dollars. . . ."

The young man's tone became hostile. Roger listened and reached for his glasses to get a read on the lawyer's face. I wasn't sure where this was going, but it felt to me like this gentleman had a major ax to grind. He then went on to say that it was CEOs like Roger who were taking advantage of American workers. That raised the fury in me because by donating his annual salary to his own workers' families—money out of his own pocket—Roger Enrico was a hero influencing other CEOs to address income inequality within the ranks of their businesses.

This was my mentor who had just been savagely attacked.

It was untrue! My jaw clenched. Just then, Roger Enrico, who once had the ambition of being an actor and who had an ability to electrify a room that I'd witnessed many times, cleared his throat. In this instance, he spoke barely above a normal speaking voice as he said, "You have neither a question nor a request. What you have, sir, is an opinion. And you and I can debate this opinion anytime. We're just not going to do it today."

It was a classic Roger Enrico mic drop. Everyone sat in silence. Something else needed to be said. And I needed to say it. It was impromptu. But I felt that I had been preparing to say it all my life.

I'm not sure how long it took me to get up to the stage but I had to give my name to the secretary who knew me and who looked up questioningly—*You, you're going to speak?* When my name was announced, Roger also looked up with surprise.

As I reached the mic, I greeted everyone, thanked the CEO for his earlier recognition of me, and thanked the shareholders, promising I would take only a moment of their time. "As you heard, my name is Richard Montañez, and I'm from Southern California, where I work in a Frito-Lay plant as a PMO." I paused to explain that a PMO was a packaging machine operator. I went on: "And for those of you who don't know what a PMO does . . . that's the guy who puts the chips in the bag."

Everyone laughed and applauded.

"You know," I continued, "it's been a privilege for me to be able to do that and to have been employed at this plant over twenty years. I know not everyone is impressed with what I do. I remember somebody made the comment once about my being a PMO. That person said to me, 'It's not rocket science.'"

The room became quiet again.

I spoke directly to the shareholders. "'Let me tell you something about rocket science.' That's what I said to that person. And I asked him, 'You know who Neil Armstrong is, don't you?' He said yes. And I said, 'You know he went to the moon,' and he said yes. 'Well,' I said to him, 'Neil Armstrong has never been able to put a chip in a bag.'"

Everyone roared.

That was enough of a reception for me to go on. "Ladies and gentlemen, now is not the time to get rid of any stock because I'm telling you from the front line, we are geared up and ready to have a record-setting year ahead."

As it happened, they had the entire meeting playing on the loudspeaker throughout Frito-Lay headquarters. Well over three thousand employees had listened in and heard the line about Neil Armstrong never putting a chip in a bag. Everyone in the entire complex came running out of their offices—from marketing, sales, supplies, and all the R & D people too.

Everyone who didn't have a big title or a high-level position was empowered, maybe even electrified. As a leader, I had experienced a rite of passage. The stage was set and the words were there when I needed them. That day I think a lot of future Deliverers found their voices.

The secret that I'm happy to share with you is that this was a leadership moment about doing the right thing and speaking out on someone else's behalf. Doing what's right—when it's not easy and when you've never done anything like it before—can be transformative. When you really need to speak up and take a stand based on the courage of your convictions, you'll be amazed that you can be given the moment, the words, the electric power, and the opportunities to do so. Sometimes the choice to act on your convictions can be the moment when you become a true leader.

Whatever else was going to happen, I came to the conclusion that I had expressed my great appreciation and that it was time for me to move on. Expressing my gratitude on a public platform of that size seemed to have balanced the scales. And so I accepted an offer at a small manufacturing company and looked forward to starting a new chapter. After all, that's what leaders do.

The immediate response when I notified Steve Reinemund was that there had to have been a mistake. "We thought you were happy?" He had no idea that the offer had never been presented to me. Steve asked me not to make a final decision about taking a job elsewhere until he had time to talk to HR and others who would want to chime in on a counteroffer.

In the end, I decided not to leave. Without further ado, they made me a manager and created the position of community business development manager, which had not existed before, at least not at Frito-Lay, and then threw me out into the ocean again so I could figure out how to swim back to shore one more time.

Really, it was a gift. More than ever I got to act like an

owner without encountering too many negative responses. Not only that, but, apparently, my job was going to allow me to help a lot of people in the community. Judy was relieved when I got home and gave her the news. "What does a community business development manager do?" she asked.

"No idea," I answered. I thought about it some more and proposed, "I guess whatever needs to get done."

Judy, leader that she is, just inspired and encouraged me, and reminded me, "You'll have a revelation."

ONE MORE ASPECT OF LEADERSHIP THAT DOESN'T GET THE ATTENTION it deserves is Leadership Lesson Number Four—working for the greater good, or what I call *serving as a connector*. When you create opportunities for yourself that benefit you, your fellow employees, your company, along with other companies and groups of people, that is being a connector.

Serving as a connector has been one of the most satisfying parts of my leadership journey.

Most everyone seemed to think that my role as manager of business development was just to put a face to the local Frito-Lay business and give out free money to needy organizations and educational institutions in the community. Not at all. That's strictly philanthropy and comes from the nonprofit foundation that most corporations use for improving their corporate image.

My concept for community *business* development was to create partnerships between Frito-Lay, community-based organizations, and local/national retailers. It kind of developed organically after I attended a conference for leaders of CBOs (community-based organizations) and got to know some of the social activists in the poor Latino and African American communities. Their organizations included educational and literacy programs, job training, antipoverty efforts, food banks, children's hospitals, and other social philanthropies. Frito-Lay had already allotted a lot of money to a program at California State, Los Angeles, with the idea of creating educational scholarships and then offering jobs to the graduates of the program at our plants and in our offices. To run that, they gave me an office I used part-time on campus. But my own model of making money for our bottom line wasn't being met. If I was spending more on my salary and on helping to get money circulating in communities and among businesses in those neighborhoods but wasn't bringing in that much or more in revenues, I was falling short.

So then it occurred to me that many of the employees of local retailers (stores that sold our products) had never been to college. This was a revelation pure and simple. *What if,* I asked myself, we created training for them on the college campus that could give them basic business skills—say, an eight-week course that covered marketing, accounting, and so on, complete with a certificate awarded at the end? The store owners and managers loved it. We were investing in and enriching the lives of the students served by the community-based education/job training organization, *and* investing in and educating the retail employees and the stores themselves. So it was logical that we'd want an investment in return that would lead to added shelf space, and more of our product sold.

The only benchmark I had for measuring success was whether enrollment and employment went up for students, whether our retailers' business increased, and whether we had incremental sales from those communities. Incremental, as I'd learned in the beginning, means we are seeing sales numbers move up steadily, bit by bit. Staying level, or tracking the same earnings week to week, was not a sustainable business model. We looked for incremental growth. That's good for our bottom line. The way that I communicated this new paradigm was to break it down into three stages: (1) social philanthropy, (2) community development, and (3) retail activation.

Let's say you are the Salvation Army and you are building a new wing to a facility. Instead of giving you $100,000 for your building fund and having our name on the banner at your fundraising gala, we would partner with our local Food for Less and give them the money to donate to you. They would also get the signage and the bump in local business from other supporters of the Salvation Army. We would also work with the leadership of the Salvation Army to lend our organizational expertise to help put that money to good use. So the social philanthropy was giving to a good cause and the community development was helping that cause maximize their resources, and the retail activation was seeing our partner, Food for Less, expand their inventory of our products. Our $100,000 would yield millions in incremental sales.

The way I promoted it to our retail partners was to say that we were investing in their livelihoods and educations and in their children's. If our competitors were doing that and more, I would say, by all means give them my shelf space. But if they weren't and we were making a difference, then I wanted their shelf space.

Many of these strategic alliances became commonplace in later years. At the time I was out in the hood making my moves, they were revolutionary. My self-created job was so successful that it was duplicated throughout nine regions of the country, creating nine other managerial positions like mine.

On your leadership journey, when you choose to serve as a connector, you can reap real dividends. It was great to be acknowledged around this time when I somehow became known as the Godfather of Hispanic Marketing (and Branding). That name was publicly given to me in 2003, when I spoke at a luncheon for Telemundo (the Spanish-language cable network), and that's how the emcee introduced me as I came up to the podium. The name stuck.

It was exciting to connect to other leaders in the Latin community who had inspired me over the years and to celebrate our arrival as an important economic force in our country. Not many people knew my story of having started as a janitor, although I proudly wore my barrio beginnings on my sleeve.

Finally, in 2005, at long last, no doubt as the result of my rising profile, I was promoted to a vice president of PepsiCo. Thanks to Al Carey, who oversaw sales and marketing for Pepsi, I was brought in to work with his heads of marketing around the country and to do for Pepsi (and all the beverage brands) what I had done at Frito-Lay.

This was to be the most challenging work I'd ever undertaken and also the most fun. The hard part had to do with the fact that unlike Frito-Lay, which had no true competitor, Pepsi was still number two in many markets or not even that high in some. That meant marketing and sales almost had to mount a stealth campaign to convey how flamin' hot it was to drink our beverages—based on how awesome and diverse our retailers and consumers were. Not by advertising but by serving as a connector and being relevant to communities through wealth creation strategies.

How does a leader inspire a brand to develop wealth creation strategies? The first thing I did was to gather my field generals who oversaw sales to retailers in communities of color, and we set up in-person visits. Old-fashioned knocking on doors. Retailers loved it. They had never even met the regional head of sales in their area. We cultivated partnerships with retailers and the community-based organizations they saw as needing help. Much of what we accomplished came from conversations—talking and listening to their needs and aspirations.

Even though I had once questioned the importance of a title or a high-level position, I was proud to become the first Latino to achieve executive status. As a revolutionary leader and Deliverer, I could now claim that I had truly made it all the way from the barrio to the boardroom.

In 2012, I was given an award presented by the Amer-

ican Latino Media Arts (ALMA) Foundation for being a positive role model and for encouraging corporate America to
increase outreach to diverse communities, as well as for my
work with the National Council of La Raza (now known as
UnidosUS) to gain greater recognition for the growing market influence of Latinos.

Accompanied to the ALMA awards ceremony by Al Carey,
I had to laugh at how far I'd come from the day long ago when
I broke ranks to introduce myself to him. And now here we
were, riding in a limousine, dressed in tuxedos, on our way to
attend a star-studded affair where I would be honored.

Remember when my coworkers mocked me for wearing
clothes that were above my station, and I told them that up-
grading my wardrobe was my way of practicing to become my
future self? Can you imagine how ridiculous it would have
been to predict that one day I'd be riding in a limo dressed in
a tux, hanging out with the CEO on our way to an award for
me? That just goes to prove once more how your future can be
shaped by the courage to appear or sound ridiculous.

A short while after the awards event, *People* magazine
printed a shot of me on the red carpet and captioned it, "As
PepsiCo's top Latino executive Montañez has been invited to
speak and kick off Hispanic Heritage Month events at Fortune
100 companies that include Wal MART AND Kroger [*sic*]."

Almost immediately I received an irate email from our
communications office chastising me for claiming a title that
wasn't true.

"Look," I said, "I can't tell *People* magazine what to write."

Honestly, I was the top Latino executive at the time but didn't want to argue it. The response came back that they just wanted to reserve that accolade possibly for someone else.

I sat there looking at that statement for all of two minutes and then let it go. Al Carey actually laughed, agreeing that it was not an issue of concern. Julius C. McGee, my earliest mentor—who had never been given his due—was even more delighted that I'd made it to the big time. *People* magazine was proof to him that I had not sold myself short for a steak dinner.

Along the road to becoming comfortable as a leader, by the way, I had some awkward moments. Many times I had to ask Julius how to prepare for VIP events that were new to me. He'd advise on everything from appropriate dress and etiquette to how to carry myself during the seven times I was invited to the White House, where I met every president from George Herbert Walker Bush to Barack Obama, plus vice presidents, senators, congressional representatives, governors, mayors, and city council members.

Every now and then, no prep helped me. There was the first time, for instance, that Roger Enrico invited me to New York for a commercial shoot and then for a flight from there to Washington, DC, to the White House for a state dinner hosted by President Bush and First Lady Barbara Bush. The part that made me the most nervous was flying on a company jet for the first time. This was in the days before cell phones, so I couldn't call anyone for advice. At the airport, when I got to the area for private jets, nobody told me how to check my suitcase— and of course I had overpacked with a large suitcase I brought into the jet with me. None of the flight personnel said anything, so I kept the suitcase with me, and being the first to arrive, I took a seat near the front.

As several of the executives boarded the flight, I noticed that none of them had luggage. Each of them saw the seat I'd chosen and gave me a strange look, but nobody said anything. Just, "Oh, hi Richard, great to see you." Someone did say, "Oh, you're sitting in the front seat," as if I were the guy who called "shotgun."

Nobody came right out and said that I was sitting in the CEO's seat. When Roger Enrico arrived, he gave me a warm greeting and went to take one of the seats farther back. Someone finally did offer to take my luggage down to where they were stowing all the bags.

Much later, the vice president of HR was the one who was kind enough to tell me that the front seat of the private jet is reserved for the CEO or whoever is the most senior executive on the flight. Out of respect for me, no one had said anything, but I needed to know the protocol.

When I reported my cluelessness to Judy, she reminded me that the mistake was a blessing because now I would know better the next time. How could she be so sure there would be a next time to fly in the private jet? She gave me that look that said, "Have I ever been wrong?"

My first White House visit was unforgettable. President George Herbert Walker Bush was gracious, down-to-earth, and told some good jokes. First Lady Barbara Bush exuded warmth and leadership. The whole time I was there I tried to soak up every detail so I could share everything with Judy and the kids when I got home. At a gathering in the Rose Garden before the dinner, I grabbed a handful of the elegant paper napkins that bore the insignia of the White House and acted as if I were going to wipe the sweat off my face. Instead, I put them in my pocket to take home and show the family.

At every subsequent visit—with President Bill Clinton, President George W. Bush, and President Barack Obama—I felt more and more at home. It's not like I'm going to run for office anytime soon. But then again, you never know. After all, why not?

On the other visits, I wasn't able to grab any presidential paper napkins like the first time. Instead, I couldn't resist picking up a cloth hand towel from the bathroom to take home to prove to my skeptical coworkers, friends, and family that I had legitimately been to the White House. Though I'm embarrassed to admit liberating those cloth towels, I hear it's such a common occurrence that most White House staffs make them specifically available for guests to quietly take home.

During my last visit to the White House, during President Obama's second term, I had the pleasure of bringing Judy with me, and I have to say that seeing her there, her eyes shining bright and looking like a million dollars or more, I knew we definitely were at a place where we could savor and enjoy the fruits of our labor. For two kids from the hood, we had escaped poverty and had achieved the American dream—not unlike Barack and Michelle Obama.

That night, I experienced a first when I became the first

person in the history of the world to be served Flamin' Hot Cheetos in the White House Blue Room.

Maybe you're thinking that you could easily experience all that my family and I have enjoyed on your own terms, with your own life. If so, let your leadership adventure begin. If not, if you are worried about your situation or if you feel hesitant about what it takes to lead, perhaps you can find a leader who can tell you how she or he made it. There is always hope, always a new idea and a new day to launch a revelation that's going to take you all the way from the barrio to the boardroom to the Blue Room of the White House.

Hopefully I've been able to encourage, inspire, and remind you of the natural leadership gifts that I might never have believed were in me, but that I know wholeheartedly are in you. A quick review:

* You can be a leader at any stage, even at the ground floor, when you work for the benefit of others, using your words and your voice on their behalf.
* Your success will breed success in others. Share your success story with someone else and be a blessing to that person in your example.
* When you lead, why be run-of-the-mill? Go flamin' hot and dare to electrify those who need a jolt, sharing a portion of your energy with them.
* While you choose to invest in the success of others, remember it's also important to speak up on your own behalf when you feel you have not gotten the compensation or promotions you deserve.

* Look around you to identify the difference between Pharaohs and Deliverers. Choose which one you want to be by helping and empowering those around you.
* Look for opportunities to serve as a connector at work, in your neighborhood, and in your community. How can you serve the greater good?
* Take the leadership ride and see where and how far it can take you, always making sure to bring others along with you.

Suffice it to say, I don't think my ability to turn a revelation into a revolution would have been possible without belief at some core level that I had it in me. Let me quickly add that nothing at all would have been possible to accomplish without the most important leader in life—my wife, Judy.

If I've said it once or twice or even three times, I have to say it again before we move on. Nothing can compare with the leadership of a woman. And you don't have to give me credit if you ever want to quote me—God was definitely showing off the day he created woman.

10

Believe That There Is Greatness in You

No matter how many times you're given an important message, until you are ready to hear it, the words will sound like static in your ears. When you're ready, you'll hear them spoken as if for the first time—like the "Hallelujah Chorus."

The message I most want to give you is that *You are meant for greatness.* Once you believe that there is greatness in you, right now, that mind-set will spark your most creative and inspired ideas. No matter how hungry, passionate, purposeful, and hardworking you are, if you don't believe you are meant for greatness—if you believe that life's never been fair or that you're not gifted or not even very smart—you will undoubtedly not get very far.

How do you learn to believe? Sometimes you have to do as we did earlier and go back to your past to know your future.

I'll bet that as you've looked at the key moments of your journey, you may not have given yourself credit where credit has been deserved. Maybe in looking back again, you'll recall ways that you applied belief in some form or fashion that you can now choose to use to identify the greatness that's inside of you.

Hopefully, you may have had family members and loved ones who saw your value and believed in you before you saw your own possibilities. That was my story. I was fourteen years old when Judy and I first met. She was beautiful, radiant, with a smile that lit up a room, and I was trouble. We both came from the hood, but she had grown up on the slightly better side of the tracks. There wasn't much time to really get to know each other, as this was during that same period when I was arrested for truancy and eventually carted off to a juvenile detention camp. Every time I'd get out of lockup or had been off on one of my adventures, we'd see each other at parties here and there, and talk about music or cars. I loved classic cars, and because my dad could fix anything right out of the junk heap, I must have boasted about the cool lowriders and Harleys I was going to have one day. (Spoiler alert: Currently, I have more than a few tricked-out custom classic and sports cars, along with my Harley.)

From the earliest days, Judy had a wonderful laugh and thought I was funny. She was fun too, and even though I could tell she was way smarter than me, she didn't seem to take anything too seriously. Later I found out her situation at home wasn't easy either and that she wanted to escape the poverty and dysfunction of her environment and to get more out of life than what was in front of her at that time. We kissed on one or two occasions, but that was the extent of it.

At seventeen, back again and determined to stay out of trouble, I ran into Judy, who had blossomed into a young woman and, wow, that was it. Why ramble around looking for anyone else when she was right in front of me? We were both on our own, both surviving, though barely, when we moved in together and conceived our first child. My fighting days were not over, and I can tell you that she saved my life more than once by pulling me back from the edge. I probably saved her life too.

We didn't plan on spacing out the boys to have one every six years, but it was a blessing we did because each of our sons brought a new level and kind of prosperity. Richard junior, our first, got the nickname "Lucky" in honor of my father, whose name is Luciano—like Lucky Luciano the gangster. What's in a name? You never know, but Lucky looks completely Italian American.

Interestingly enough, for all the years that my dad had not been able to articulate affection and pride, the arrival of my son changed everything.

My father was so excited about his grandson because he could do things for him that he couldn't do for his kids, maybe. One day I'll never forget, at a point when I was still trying to figure out my future as a teenage parent, my dad had come to see the baby and said to me, "Son, I've never had to worry about you." He paused and said words to me he'd never spoken, "I love you, Ricardo."

Two years later when I got the job as janitor at Frito-Lay,

my dad and my grandfather were the first to hear the news, and their wisdom remains the most important guidance I could have received at the start and then be able to pass on as a legacy to my kids and grandkids. When you choose to mop the floors so well that all who see it will know that a Montañez did it, you become an owner of your life. When you work for your name—not your boss, not your paycheck, not the "plantations"—you are leading your own wealth revolution.

To this day, every single one of my three kids and my five grandkids carries on the legacy of the Montañez name. That message to me, like the message my father sent by telling me that he loved me, was pivotal, without a doubt. It wasn't until we were expecting our second son, Steven, that I actually started to believe I was capable of creating the life I wanted for our family. Up until then, I was that janitor trying to make my way and starting to climb the rocks, but I still wanted to party and get into fights like in the old days.

The notion that I had greatness in me was out of reach. Poverty had been a fact of life for a good part of my life. What many who haven't experienced it don't understand is that when you're born into poverty, it can become a generational curse. For the family that raised me, every generation on both parents' sides had lived in poverty for the last one hundred years. Once, I remember, we visited relatives who lived in New Mexico with no hot water and the bathroom outside— which was kind of scary to use, to say the least. My relatives never complained.

In my family, we were taught by my parents and elected leaders to survive poverty. We were shown where the welfare office was and how to apply for food stamps and the best way to get an extension on your utility bill. We were not taught a method of escape. We were not taught where to apply for college or how to get a library card and the ways to look up information for escaping poverty. We were not taught that we all have entrepreneurship in our DNA and that if we are willing to do the work, we can apply for a business loan from the Small Business Administration.

I believe in all forms of help, governmental and private. In fact, as someone who has escaped poverty and achieved wealth, I gladly pay my taxes to make sure we have safety nets to prevent people from falling below the poverty line. We still can do more across the board to empower poorer citizens to succeed. We have to stop making it profitable to put minors and adults in jail when what they could really use is literacy and job training. As a living example, I am the first to say that kids shouldn't be judged as bad because they come from bad environments. They, too, need to be helped to do more than survive those environments.

Before I came up with my own poverty escape plan, I observed the contrasting dreams that are common to the haves and the have-nots. Generally speaking, poor people dream of money. Rich people dream of things. Wealthy people are the ones who dream of ideas.

All of this was made clear to me once Judy and I became parents. On a particular night when Lucky was about seven and Steven was not quite two years old, we were getting ready to go trick-or-treating in an area where the houses were bigger and the candy was obviously going to be better and more plentiful. We were headed out and I remembered all the years of my childhood when I used to go trick-or-treating on the rich side of town too. We had to cross the tracks to get there, but that's what you did if you wanted to get the good candies. We'd start going door-to-door and all I could do was peek inside and dream—*How do you get a house like this?* Poverty would answer back, telling me that I wasn't good enough, smart enough, white enough, or worthy of being able to one day have a house like that.

As Judy and I set off for trick-or-treating with our sons, I suddenly understood that we were going across town so the boys could see what they weren't supposed to want to have if they were just going to carry on the legacy of survival. The answer appeared. To escape poverty, I had to own my life even more, envision the future I wanted to live, and create opportunities to do so out of my imagination. The time had come to enact the escape plan by leaving the land of *not enough* and travel next into the land of *barely enough*, knowing that we would arrive before long to the promised land of *more than enough*.

Our wealth revolution started in my mind. When I then learned to act like an owner at work, I began my family's great escape from poverty. Remember, you can take your nothing and turn it into something. You can take your current condition and use it to determine your future position.

And yet, I will tell you now that I hadn't really begun to believe the things that I hoped would happen. There was still a part of me that didn't want responsibilities, didn't want to grow up.

Around that time, Judy had begun attending a local church and had started to make different choices for herself. Her spiritual growth was for herself because she owned her own life, and she never insisted that I seek the same path. She said very little by way of judgment. That is, until one night when I had gotten into a fight with a friend, and Judy calmly said in the most loving way possible that the time had come for me to grow up.

In so many words she said—*You're better than this.*

I wanted to believe her, but even with the accomplishments at work and the sense of ownership that I did have, I was impatient for change. Maybe she was just saying that I had good ideas but really didn't go anywhere with them.

Judy told me there was so much more to be revealed that I was going to do. She spoke with so much heart and love, and had always shown that she had a strong sense of intuition. "Richard, you're not like anyone else; I know you," she said and then read a passage from her Bible from Proverbs. It said, "Do you see a man skilled in his work? He will be stationed in the presence of kings; he will not stand before obscure men."

The words sounded good, but whatever the fight had been about, it was still in my mind.

Judy dug her heels in. She insisted that she could see me walking through doors and into hallowed halls that none of us had ever imagined and that I would sit with people from high places who would look to me for my knowledge. Her pep talk worked. Shortly after that I, too, started attending church and having my own spiritual awakening. Whoever said that you can lead a horse to water but you can't make him drink was wrong. They had never met my wife.

Judy saw it and told me, Julius believed I was a diamond in the rough, and my father and grandfather believed. Yet it wasn't until I agreed to begin attending church services with Pastor Ernie at a large church in our area that I could hear what they were trying to say to me. One of the enticements was the fact that this church in the hood offered educational classes that didn't necessarily emphasize the Bible or religion. If it was some kind of school, I was pretty sure they'd kick me out; in the past I'd been told that I was unteachable. So I figured what the heck, if it's a church, they have to let me in, and besides, it can't hurt to have God on my side. That thought made me more receptive to classes, but it wasn't until Pastor Ernie started working with me as a teacher and friend that I was able to shed the shame and baggage of twenty-two years enough to be able to accept his belief.

At our second meeting, Pastor Ernie told me, "Richard, I see greatness in you." With that, he handed me back a book report I'd written for him and to my shock, I looked down at the paper and there at the top, in ink, was a large letter A. For the first time in my life, I'd received an A. First he says he sees greatness in me, then he gives me an A, and then he says, "You have a spirit of excellence."

You know what? That got me. Because I knew it to be true. My striving for excellence in my work had proved that to me. So now I found it tempting and somewhat easier to believe that maybe I could have some greatness in me. A little?

Pastor Ernie continued to give me assignments, suggesting

books about subjects he could see would be of interest. This gave me increased confidence—which is a word worth studying as you embrace your greatness and your hotness:

> confidence (*n.*) c. 1400, "assurance or belief in the good will, veracity, etc. of another," from Old French *confidence* or directly from Latin *confidentia* . . . "firmly trusting, bold." . . .
>
> From mid-15c as "reliance on one's own powers, resources, or circumstances, self-assurance." Meaning "certainty of a proposition or assertion, sureness with regard to a fact" is from 1550s. Meaning "a secret, a private communication" is from 1590s.*

Two things happened at that point. For starters, I began to work at self-belief, as much for my kids as for me. If I could set an example of self-confidence and a belief that I was meant for greatness, they would model those beliefs. My conclusion was that our job is not to seek others whose wisdom will put the greatness into us, but rather to seek those who will help us get our greatness out. This process was extremely helpful at tuning out the voices of those who were threatened by my greatness.

Acting like an owner helped me flex those muscles of belief. This was my way of learning to *faith it till you make it*. Notice I didn't say to fake it till you make it. Why? Because

---

Online Etymology Dictionary, s.v. "confidence (*n.*)," www.etymonline
.com/word/confidence.

"faking it" suggests you don't believe it and that you are just going to trick yourself and others. "Faith it till you make it" is based on the premise that you believe you are meant for greatness and are taking a leap of faith that the things that make you special and different haven't yet been revealed. "Faith it till you make it" takes the pressure off.

Greatness has been inside you since you were born. It is your true wealth, your inheritance, your destiny. Your job is to value it and take righteous, courageous action toward putting it to use.

MY DECISION TO RETIRE FROM PEPSICO TOWARD THE END OF 2019 HAD not been a difficult one to make. For the most part, my main mentors and champions had moved on. On June 1, 2016, I received the news that Roger Enrico had suffered a heart attack while snorkeling in the Cayman Islands. This was his second. The first had been a mild one and it had motivated him to stop smoking. But he didn't recover from this second heart attack. He was only seventy-one years old—young by today's standards. His death was devastating for me. My dad had died in a similarly sudden way, and with both of them gone, I felt a big void in my life. Roger was always a phone call away, the second person (after Judy) whose reaction and feedback to my newest ideas were so vital. I remembered that Roger had been ambivalent at one time about staying at the helm of PepsiCo. His real passion was mentorship, and he always planned on doing more of it once he slowed down.

It had already occurred to me that the time would come when I'd be ready to focus on my own company and expand my reach as a mentor—passing on the lessons I'd learned from the greats who had helped bring out the greatness inside me.

To that end, the examples I've shared wouldn't be complete if I didn't include lessons in greatness learned from Indra Nooyi, not only the first woman CEO in PepsiCo's history but also, as an immigrant who was born in India, the first CEO at PepsiCo to have firsthand experience of the changing impact of globalization on the new global marketplace. Unlike her predecessors, she understood diversity from a lived experience, and she drew from those insights as she moved the company forward with ease.

Both intellectually and spiritually, Indra taught me about making evenhanded decisions. She was tough but in an understated way. Early in her tenure, there was a story about Indra that had to do with an overseas tour—the sort that regularly took our CEOs and an entourage to visit remote retail outlets for our products, typically involving many hours of travel over uncomfortable terrain. As the story goes, when she was getting into a van, a door was closed on her fingers, but she brushed it off, saying she was fine. For the rest of the day, she didn't complain at all, but later that night back at the hotel, she realized her pain was so acute she had to make a visit to the emergency room at a local hospital for her broken fingers. I'm not sure I would have held out all day.

Indra could be extremely decisive—as she had to be to overhaul the product line, breaking it into more health-conscious categories. Yet Indra was a marvelous listener who made everyone feel that their voice counted and mattered. She had a gift for identifying gifts in others.

Not long after she arrived, I began to write a series of motivational emails that I would send out to a list of about a hundred thousand of our employees and to another even longer list of my own that included our strategic partners. There were always one or two people who would write me to say, "Drop me from the list." I understood. Not everybody wants daily motivation.

Most everyone else loved my emails. Chief among them was Indra. "Oh, Richard," she'd tell me. "You can be writing for hundreds of thousands of people, but I always feel your message is just for me and just what I needed to hear."

During the financial banking collapse of 2007–2008 that precipitated the Great Recession, the chain reaction of fear had everyone freaking out.

My email theme was resilience. In it I addressed its value as a prized quality, as much to organizations as to individuals. Naturally, I delved into the word's etymology, writing about how it was originally used to describe the ability to spring back into one's original form.

Resilience, I wrote, was once a scientific term from discoveries that everything has a breaking point with a bounce back into position or original state. Writing to our employees, I said, "We have such great power in our brands but the resilience of our company is our people/strength, which each one of you carry. The ability to bounce back from a negative situation. The ability to return to your original shape after being compressed or stretched."

In hindsight, while I was speaking to that time in the world, we all should know that resilience is timeless and the conversation is as needed now as it was then. Maybe more.

"Resilience," I wrote, "is that ineffable quality that allows some people to be knocked down by life and come back stronger than ever. Rather than letting failure overcome them and drain their resolve, they find a way to rise from the ashes. Some of my good friends are world champion boxers, and I have learned from watching them, how they get knocked down and with resilience they get back up and in many cases go on to win the fight."

My mentors, the leaders I have known, and my own kids have taught me that in the toughest of times you can choose, instead of a comeback, to be a *bounceback*. You get up and bounce back into it! And remember, if you've never been knocked down, you haven't been in a fight.

Resilience is literally the art of the *bounceback*, the *springback*, or the *jumpback*. The resilience test in the eighteenth century was used to test the strength of steel—its bounce, its flexibility, its capacity to spring back even after being bent almost to the breaking point. That's what the resilience of your steel can do. That's where greatness lies.

My conversations with Indra about corporate and organizational resilience were fascinating, unforgettable. It was as if I were getting a postdoctorate in leadership. But then, not long after Roger Enrico died, Indra prepared to leave. And in

2018, Al Carey announced he was going to be moving on. Many of the new breed of executives knew me and my story, but they didn't know of the strategies and paradigm shifts that had been made possible by my partnerships with all the CEOs no longer at the helm.

Unlike some who think corporations have become too big and have swallowed up too many of the smaller competitors, I believe in the productivity and wealth creation potential of great corporations like PepsiCo. There is always room for improvement and the humanization and democratization of corporate entities, absolutely. But in times of economic hardship, corporations have the potential to energize, support, and uplift communities and individuals in need. I'm proud to have pioneered some of those practices.

My new life post-PepsiCo has inspired me to look for stories, in addition to my own, that amplify the message that we all have greatness inside. My favorites are stories of people who have been broken only to discover the gold within that is revealed from the cracks. There is a Japanese process called *kintsugi* that involves taking pieces of broken pottery, reassembling the bowl or pot, and painting over the broken places with paint made of gold dust. Each piece of repaired pottery is a masterpiece, even more beautiful and special than it was before. This is a reminder that your breaks and your scars do not mar your greatness—they enhance it.

Another story I've always loved is about Rebecca Webb Carranza, who pioneered the making of tortilla chips. She had been in the tortilla-making business and one day picked up a round taco shape and it broke in her hands. She started toasting the tortillas and breaking them on purpose. Needless to say, that revelation caused a major revolution. She went on to start other companies with other ideas after losing her chip business in a divorce. Not long ago, Rebecca passed away at ninety-eight, and up to the end she was still working on developing new ideas. Talk about the leadership and greatness of a woman—without whom the world would be a colder and less delicious place for sure.

I love the parable of the wealthy man who lived in the Middle East (in what is now Iraq) who drew all of his happiness from being rich. A priest visited him and said he should have diamonds to be truly rich. The man lusted for diamonds and became convinced he was poor because he didn't have them, even though that wasn't the case. He ended up selling his many acres of land and going off in search of diamonds. Finding none, he grew depressed and lost his will to live, ultimately throwing himself into the sea.

Meanwhile, the man who bought his land made the surprising discovery one day of a handful of diamonds in the riverbed. Lo and behold, there were acres of diamonds that he was able to unearth and harvest. The moral that I like is that a lot of us think our fortunes and our greatness can only come to fruition elsewhere when really we already have what it takes to create opportunities right where we are—just under our feet.

Along these same lines is the story of the Golden Buddha that was discovered in Thailand in the 1950s. For years a huge, ugly concrete Buddha had sat in the middle of the town square in Bangkok. Visitors threw trash on it and had no sense of its value. At a certain point, a monk arranged for it to be moved to a nearby temple, and in the process it fell and cracked. At the temple, the monk spotted something underneath the concrete. He and some helpers chiseled off the concrete shell and found the world's largest piece of sculpted gold underneath—a Buddha that was almost eight feet tall.

My interpretation is that a lot of us have that gold underneath, and it may take some shaking and banging up for our value to be revealed. On a spiritual level, our higher power—however you choose to define that entity—knows of our gifts and potential and is waiting for us to believe there is greatness inside in order to help transform our life for the better. There may come a time when you choose to let go of those pieces of concrete to reveal the gold underneath, the trash that maybe others threw on you that has covered up your greatness. Begin by believing and the revelation will follow.

The leadership story about greatness within that Pastor Ernie shared with me long ago and one I return to again and again to gain new insights is the Biblical story of David and Goliath. Everyone loves to talk about this story, but there are some details that often get overlooked. It is well established that David was not the likeliest candidate to become king. The first king of Israel was Saul, and he was famously the tallest warrior and the handsomest king ever. Only he wasn't a great king. God wanted to choose his successor and sent Samuel, the prophet, to the home of Jesse, who had a lot of sons, including David—who was not the tallest or even the handsomest. David, a shepherd, was ostensibly not an able warrior, although what's often overlooked is that he had fought off lions and bears to protect his sheep. Still, Jesse didn't know the great-ness of his own son David and didn't even bother calling him for Samuel to consider as a candidate for king. None of Jesse's other sons impressed Samuel, who then thought to ask if Jesse had any other sons. Begrudgingly, Jesse called for David.

When Samuel saw David's greatness, God confirmed that the shepherd boy was the one He wanted for king.

That's the first we learn about David's having greatness that is yet to be revealed. God sees it, but no one else does. What happens next is the part of the story that also gets overlooked, when the giant Goliath decides to wreak terror on the king-dom. He doesn't challenge just anyone to fight him. Goliath, who the Bible tells us is more than nine feet tall and rippling with muscles, puts the challenge to King Saul, known as the greatest warrior in the land. Guess what! Saul had never seen anyone bigger than himself and flat out refuses to fight him.

When David heard that the great and mighty king didn't want to fight Goliath, he asked for the job—knowing full well that nobody else would want it. He saw it as an opportunity to prove himself. "This is my giant!" David insisted.

Ridiculous, right? Well, we know now that greatness often comes in ridiculous forms, and here you have a classic exam-ple. This had to be crazy to everyone. But nobody else wanted to fight the giant. David knew that slaying Goliath and end-ing his wave of terror was how this future king was going to change his own life.

Goliath demanded that Saul send out a champion (a surro-gate) because Saul had chickened out and wouldn't compete against Goliath. We all know how the giant must have reacted when David walked out onto the battlefield, a small apparently unassuming shepherd without armor. The Bible says that David refused to put on Saul's armor, perhaps because he had never fit into it before and perhaps because he wanted to remain agile. Something about his strategy exuded confidence. The interesting detail to me was that David approached Goliath with a wooden staff that obscured the slingshot and the stones—possibly a distraction from the real weapon.

This reminds us that your value is not in what can be seen but in what can't be seen. According to various interpretations, the staff was not only what he used to herd the sheep but traditionally shepherds would carve their great accomplishments onto the base of the staff—a testimony to their identity. David probably carried his staff as a reminder to himself of who he was and of his name, his legacy.

Maybe it gave him courage and balance. Or disarmed Goliath into thinking he could smash David to bits with one blow. We will never know, of course, because David whipped out his slingshot and with one stone strategically shot right between Goliath's eyes, slaying the giant with that one powerful shot.

David didn't listen to the naysayers. He acted like the owner of his destiny and asked the classic "what if" question. What if I stood up to the giant with my wits and with strategy, and won? He refused to stay in the line of being the last one considered as the future king. He got into the line for heroes and legends.

And that's where I'll leave you.

My question to you is, what if you stop worrying about the

detractors, get out of your comfort zone, seize your moment, let your greatness guide you, and go slay a giant of your own? What if you called that giant out and let it be known that you've got what it takes?

When you let yourself adopt the attitude that you are flamin' hot and that the world is waiting for you to show them what you've got, you will be amazed at the fearsome giants who will fall at your feet. Be your own champion, your own king or queen.

Believe that you are intended for greatness. I believed, and things turned out pretty well, and they most certainly can for you, starting right now—in the moment that you see what has remained unseen yet waiting for you to reveal it.

Just believe.

Acknowledgments

Working on this book has not only been a labor of love for me, but it has also been a true celebration of what can happen when a team of the best individual players comes together to deliver their very best. I am so grateful to every person who has had a hand in helping bring *Flamin' Hot* to life.

There are a handful of individuals I'd like to thank first, without whom I would not already be excitedly thinking about my next book. Let me start by expressing my gratitude to the rock stars at Dupree Miller—particularly my literary agents: Jan Miller, who believed in me and my story from the start, and Nena Madonia Oshman, who put so much heart into helping me find my publishing home and into guiding me early on.

Thank you to my son Steven Montañez, who was my in-house adviser and project manager through every stage of this book's development. When I went in search of a coauthor, Steven went right along with me and helped in the interviewing and selection process. We were really looking for someone who felt like family to us, and that turned out to be Mim Eichler Rivas. My most profound thanks to you, Mim, for your passion for the truth and for drawing stories out of me that I'd never told anyone before. You helped bring out what was hidden down deep, and showed me that what I thought was a rock of pain was actually a nugget of gold. When I read my own words on the page, I could not have been more proud or more pleased.

At Portfolio/Penguin, we again were given a gift, of working with our intrepid editor, Leah Trouwborst. Thank you, Leah, for your vison and your great enthusiasm. We would not have made it across the finish line without you. My lasting thanks also go to publisher Adrian Zackheim and to editorial director Niki Papadopoulos for your support of me and this book. Thank you to the rest of the stellar publishing team: Kimberly Meilun (editorial assistant), Tara Gilbride (vice president, director of publicity and marketing), Lillian Ball (associate publicist), Nicole McArdle (assistant director of marketing), Jen Heuer (director of art and design), Susan Johnson (copyeditor), Ryan Boyle (senior production editor), Matthew Boezi (production manager), Jessica Regione (senior managing editor), and Meighan Cavanaugh (art director).

Though I've mentioned it in this narrative, I feel forever blessed to have been able to take my three sons on the journey that I traveled from the barrio to the boardroom. Judy and I agree that we learn as much from them, and from our five grandchildren, as we imagine that they learn from us. Without their input and their reminders of some of the stories I've written about, I'm certain to have forgotten key passages. Lucky (Richard junior), our firstborn, remembers it all. Outgoing, ambitious, charismatic, he proved to be a superstar at Frito-Lay, starting in sales as a substitute driver—a job nobody wanted—but eventually working his way up to executive status in merchandising. After twenty years, he left to launch his own business and has put to use everything he ever learned.

Steven, from an early age, had a spiritual wisdom above his years, a powerful sense of intuition, and is all heart. When my side business as a public speaker, business consultant, and entertainment producer started to take off, I put Steven in charge as president, which makes me the actual CEO at last.

Mike, born a year before the launch of Flamin' Hot Cheetos, was there at the beginning when we went out as a family to all the stores and churches to help create a demand for the new product. Mike, extremely analytical, creative, and empathetic, always gravitated to wanting to help the underdogs of this world. When our family foundation created a program for donating to local groups in need of thousands of backpacks, sneakers, school supplies, and other educational materials, Mike was always looking for strategic ways to expand and collaborate with local agencies. Not surprisingly, he went on to work as a counselor at a drug and alcohol rehab facility and has recently returned to school to complete his degree as a therapist.

My loving thanks to each of my sons, your significant others, and my grandchildren. In addition, I want to express my love and appreciation for my beloved mother, whom we lost during the course of the writing of this book. My mom was beyond proud of what I had accomplished ever since the days when she encouraged me to offer a burrito to a fellow student as a way of making a friend—and later to turn the thing that made me different into a profitable business. She knew the real secret to success long before I figured it out.

Last but not least, there would be no book without my beautiful and beloved Judy. Thank you for everything.